Uljana

Subsisters:
Selected Poems

Translated from
the German
by Sophie Seita

Belladonna*

"'Two heads are better than *ohne*' writes Uljana Wolf, *ohne* meaning "without" in German. Yet these poems are the progeny of not two minds but four (at least), since both Wolf and Sophie Seita approach the original texts as well as their English versions from the dual vantage points of English and German, interlacing the slippages and misalignments between these and other languages into the poems' fabric. This is poetry as translation, translation as poetry, and echolalia of the best sort. I'm ecstatic for it."
    Mónica de la Torre

"This bi-floral or even tri-floral book of poems is for falselandy neighbouring nearspeakers who prefer to hold ear to phoneme to wit. Arranged according to the pleasures of a collaborative conversation between co-translating poets, sinuous between the structured palate and the muscular tongue, *Subsisters* coheres by means of a joyous principle of augmentation. Wolf and Seita have rendered authority moot; Value here is chosen conviviality. Lightness, charm and play clarify the discovery that all language is polylingual, all worth in shared joy only."
    Lisa Robertson

"Uljana Wolf is resistant, even immune, to standard translation approaches: an ironic, if also iconic, state of affairs for a poet who is also a noted translator, and whose poetry thinks so doubtingly about translation, and about doubling in general. Her poetry violates standard ways of speaking and writing because she regards them as complicit in political and social domination. Sophie Seita's witty and imaginative translations transfer the author's methods to new territories, take up her process anew, position themselves as the subsisters of the original. Hers is a very contemporary and a very sophisticated way of conceiving translation as composition, conversation, and—above all—play."
    Eugene Ostashevsky

Uljana Wolf

Subsisters: Selected Poems

Translated from the German by Sophie Seita

Belladonna*

CONTENTS

CONTENTS

On the Ellis Island of Language: The Multilingual Poetry of Uljana Wolf

Yoko Tawada

In German, we speak of someone's vocabulary as a "treasure of words" (*Wortschatz*). Words we know and that know us are valued treasures. Among those there are words that are hard to digest or close to one's heart. But we keep most words in our heads and although the brain is the organ for knowledge, we do not know how they are stored there. Are they arranged alphabetically or thematically? Are they categorized according to the seasons or to color, like in a horticultural encyclopedia? We certainly attempt to furnish every new language with a new treasure chest. Personally, I am anxious about mixing up the meanings of English and German words. It seems I prefer to keep a watertight wall between both languages. At least that is probably why I never heard the German word "Igel" (hedgehog) in the English word "eagle" until I read Uljana Wolf. She has managed to design a new order (or disorder) for the premises of the brain's center for speech. She is an excellent interior designer of multilingual poetry. When she elegantly connects words and thus traverses the boundaries between languages, an unexpected poetic formation appears, similar to a star formation. Millions of light years might separate the individual stars but when their light reaches us at the same time, we see them as one image.

How does Uljana choose the words that are capable of becoming stars? She is a master of resemblance. We have learned to ignore certain similarities in order to avoid confusion. The English word "bad" has nothing to do with the German "Bad" (bathroom), and the German "Brief" (letter) is not necessarily brief. But Uljana Wolf is not afraid of such confusions. On the contrary, she welcomes each confusing resemblance with open arms as an invitation to a new friendship.

When calling someone a "multilingual poet" one might imagine a poet who cherry-picks delicious words from the buffet of multiple language plates. But I imagine Uljana Wolf not so much at a buffet as at a desk crowded with dictionaries. Translation is an exciting, but also a difficult, precarious, and thankless job. Not every translator is able or willing to stand those moments of indeterminacy in which the seemingly solid meanings of the original appear to dissolve and have not yet found their counterpart in the target language. Those who linger in those moments are directly confronted with the materiality of language. Language becomes tangible on the level of the letters. An almost threatening proximity without any certainty. It has not yet been determined whether or not something that was once a word will be able to build a future in a new language. Translators who are wary of this process of uncertainty might try to reach this new language as quickly as possible and forget those moments of transition. Uljana Wolf, however, takes her time on the threshold of translation, on the Ellis Island of language.

She stays in motion when she holds onto the original language and paces ahead mimetically into a new language. What emerges is not a finished product but a certain corporeality:

> [I]t matters to me to walk alongside the original poem, i.e., to follow its running, striding, jumping, more than its riddles, answers, and callings. I do not mean objectively countable metrical feet (although those too), but the rhythmic-kinaesthetic imprint which a line of verse leaves behind with its ups and downs, its cadences, in my body. [...] Secretly I dream of leaving behind the ideal of an orderly and clean translation and instead, at the point where nothing and anything goes, of playing with a certain messiness, which has long been wreaking havoc in my poems.
> ("Faux-Amis Footprints")

Here, I imagine a radical form of translation that knows no other way but to cross over into poetry. For that, not all words in the original need to be replaced with words in the target language. For that, one need not serve the readers but represent the process of translation as an artistic act. For that, one does not need to compromise to find an answer but can leave the gaps intact. The translation's "messiness" is the mirror image to the cleansing of a national language in the brain. English words are allowed to appear in the German text but not as loanwords with a visitor's pass. In this cinema there is no firm division of labor between the original version and its subtitle. How absurd it then becomes to ask: "In which language do you think?" Do we not think in all languages simultaneously, both the ones we know and do not know? So-called false friends exist frequently between related languages; that is also why they are sometimes called "false brothers" in German. English and German are close relatives; Polish and German, too, belong to one family, namely that of the Indo-European languages. Wolf is not concerned with measuring the distance from what is originally her own. She questions precisely the concept of owning a language, which is called "mother tongue" but in reality belongs to the "fatherland." In a speech given at Humboldt University, Wolf spoke of the "false-land" as an appropriate alternative: "Now, it is true that I write in German, but despite my degree in German literature, it's not the language of the fatherland, but rather a false-landly one" ("Speech, Strangely Plotted, Because It Has No Bottom," 2014).

Proximity is sometimes more complicated than distance. Wolf's language has a suppleness that knows how to deal with a difficult proximity. Wolf writes: "in the beginning was, or, to start." "Begin" becomes "beguine" and the feet of the poem begin to dance new steps. I do not know if in the beginning there was a word, and if so, which one. But what if we began with translation instead? In the process of radical translation as poetry, any language can become my most beautiful "lengevitch."

(translated and abridged by Sophie Seita)

I.

Dust
Bunnies

To leave traces in language means to lay a trail into the unpredictable within the shared conditions of our lives.
Édouard Glissant, The Art of Translation

Against the place of home
I hold the transformations of the world—
Nelly Sachs, "In der Flucht" ["In Flight"]

11

STATIONARY

what is a domicile? a domicile is a star-
crossed ten of clubs. what is a crossing?

in the flubbed dialect of these forests
a crossing is the word tree. and why

do homelands play cards in the air? no one
ever saw the homelands go home. a tree

in the forest of neighboring languages
is a club in this suit. out of its wood

someone makes crosses on a map.
the countries fill in their domicile and

put the stationery back into its pencil
case. what is stationary? put it back.

with nelly sachs

MAPPA

was ist der wohnort? der wohnort ist
eine kreuzzehn. was ist die kreuzung?

in der verkorksten mundart der wälder
ist die kreuzung das wort baum. warum

spielen heimatländer in den lüften karten?
niemand hat die länder je nach hause gehn

sehn. ein baum im wald der nähesprache
ist im kartenspiel die zehn. aus seinem holz

werden auf der karte kreuze gemacht.
die länder tragen ihren wohnort ein

und legen die feder ins mäppchen
zurück. was ist ein mäppchen? zurück.

mit nelly sachs

"CAN YOU SHOW ME ON SE MAPPE"

we wanted to lean over this phrase like a charted city, to make
a point, create a mouthspace, myth of hear or say: hier, in this
net of tongues, one path was well-sprung, a mistake, mys-
tique. lingua franca stuck on our foreheads, almost touch-
ing and already legend: you are here, ich bin wer, a game of
routes, but whatever we said the words did not arrive. in-
stead the red lines snapped, rolling back into their very own
names: murmuring with the greek one, chartis, carta with
the italian, and karte with me, meaning my card: looks like
we're here. almost true freunde. and so we found, with the
wrong sign, our site, and the rest of the city we folded, in the
manner of this country, as they say, into maps.

"LOOK ON MY CARD"

wir wollten über diesen satz wie eine stadt uns beugen, punkt
erzeugen, mundraum, traum vom hören, oder sagen: hier, in
diesem netz aus zungen, ist ein weg gelungen, ein versehen,
verstehen. auf unseren stirnen, die sich fast berührten, klebte
lingua franca, schon legende: you are here, i am who, ein
routenspiel, doch was wir sprachen, kam nicht an. die roten
linien schnalzten, rollten sich zurück in ihre eigenen namen,
raunten mit dem griechen chartis, carta aus italien und karte,
also mir: sieht aus, als wären wir hier. almost true friends. so
fanden wir, mit falschem wort, den ort, und falteten den rest
der stadt, nach art des landes, wie man sagt, in mappen ein.

DUST BUNNIES VS WOOL MICE

we wanted to speak about little animals, to get on our
knees for the little beasts, those made of dust and gooey
fuzzle, in floorboards and cracks, shivering in gray coats,
our animals made of thin air. we wanted to whisper very
closely in your language and inside mine, tell me darling,
did you vacuum today. no, we didn't wish to alarm our crea-
tures, little like spots, are they spots, don't they have pom-
pom tails, bunny ears, or bunny tails and tom-tom ears,
didn't we want to smoke less, cough less, be less either
or. yesterday the room's nook was lonely in its dreary croak.
today it's a hoard, for tender hordes, un pont, we want, so
let's be quiet, let's eavesdrop on our knees: our little crea-
tures, how they swap their fluffy, moon-gray names.

DUST BUNNIES

wir wollten über kleine tiere sprechen, wollten auf die knie gehen für die kleinen tiere, jene aus staub und schlieren, in ritzen und dielen, jene, die in grauen fellen frieren, unsere tiere aus nichts. wir wollten auch ganz nah in deiner sprache und in meiner hauchen, sag mir liebes, hast du heute schon gesaugt. nein, wir wollten unsere tiere nicht erschrecken, klein wie flecken, sind das flecken, haben sie nicht puschelschwänze, lange löffel, oder lange schwänze, tuschelohren, wollten wir nicht weniger rauchen, weniger husten, weniger entweder oder sein. gestern war die zimmerecke einsam in ihrer knarzenden öde. heute ist sie hort, heute zärtlichen horden ein port, wir wollen also still sein, auf den knien lauschen: unsere kleinen tiere, wie sie ihre wollenen, mondgrauen namen tauschen.

DANCING DOUBLE SPEECH

i went to the tingel-tangel to angle lengevitch. in the cloak-roam every woman received a twin language with identical clothes, a dabbling double. but the mirrors showed only one of us—i gulped: cold spit, spooky skit. behind us word-rabbits scampered out of ashbery's hat. to the ballroom then, to circumdance my twin; at the bar a tassel of coffee with mrs stein. me, seeing ghosts!? a voice gasped from the niches where thinking remained a bit dunkeldeutsch: mr schleiermacher in his philosopher pajamas. a little box of watercress in front of his chest, nonplussed: sprouts on a white cloth! without soil! without roots! i wanted to ask for some seeds, but my twin bolted, cutting the rug with the man. two heads are better than *ohne*, advised mrs stein, and packed her buttons wieder ein.

DOPPELGEHERREDE

ich ging ins tingeltangel, lengevitch angeln. an der garde-
robe bekam jede eine zweitsprache mit identischen klamot-
ten, leicht gemoppeltes doppel. die spiegel aber zeigten nur
eine von uns, ich schluckte: kalte spucke, spuk. hinten hop-
pelten wortkaninchen aus ashberys hut. zum ballsaal dann,
mit meinem zwilling zirkumstanzen, am tresen ein köpfchen
kaffee mit mrs. stein. dass ich gespenster seh!, rief plötzlich
aus der nische, wo das denken dunkeldeutsch blieb, mr. veil-
maker im schlafanzug der philosophen. ein kressekästchen
vor der brust, verblüfft: wächst auf einem weißen blatte!
ohne alle erde! wurzellos! ich wollte nach paar samen fragen,
doch mein zwilling sprang, ging schwofen mit dem mann.
wer schatten hat, muss für die spots nicht sorgen, sagte mrs.
stein, packte ihre knöpfe ein.

SPEECH, WITH A CONJOINED TWIN

consider the lengevitch of a conjoined twin. consider the
obsessed oblige of a noble king: the conjoined twin (com-
manded by the king) was in command of seven languages,
but how divvied up?—three and a half tongues per twin-
head, or two times seven tongues coupled to fourteen? or
did these always-public brothers, so as not to double up but
to coax some breath-space out of the other, fork their lan-
guages in two? you for the pro-nouns, i for the quid-pro-quo
sounds. only when they muddled up their relative clauses
they got in each other's way: that looped back twenty-eight
years where it merged at the back.

bedenke die lengevitch eines koppelzwillings. bedenke die schimmerschaft des englischen königs: sieben sprachen beherrschte der vom könig beherrschte koppelzwilling, aber wie verteilt – dreieinhalb sprachen pro zwillingskopf oder zweimal sieben sprachen zu vierzehn gekoppelt? oder haben diese immer öffentlichen brüder, um sich nicht zu doppeln, um einander atemabstand zu entlocken, ihre sprachen in der mitte aufgespalten? du die fürwörter, ich die fürwas-wörter. nur bei der dehnung der selbstlaute kamen sie sich ins gehege, das war achtundzwanzig jahre lang und wuchs am rücken zusammen.

SECOND SPEECH, WITH A CONJOINED TWIN

i wonder myself if the conjoined brothers, when unable to sleep at night, because one of them had an itchy leg, but the same leg did not itch his counterpart-head, or when the spleen of one flowed over into the other's overfull sorrow-sieve—did they then translate each other, tweaking their cases with the crown-pronged dawn? and in the morning, did the king lug them onto the town square as his speech-machine, the platform creaking, and just across the early fish

> fische,
> poisson,
> poison, and did the scales bounce from the fish-

monger's blade, small headless rounds or sounds, in which, if you looked closely, first the glances vanished, then the naming, the air.

ZWEITE REDE MIT
KOPPELZWILLING

ich wunder, ob die koppelbrüder nachts, wenn sie nicht
schlafen konnten, weil einem das bein juckte, dem andern
das gleiche bein im gegenüberkopf nicht, wenn einem die
milz stieg in des andern übervolles kummersieb – ob sie ein-
ander übersetzten, am zackenkranz des dämmerns ihre fälle
wetzten? ob der könig sie als sprachmaschine auf den markt-
platz karrte, morgens, die tribüne knarzte, gegenüber die
frühen fische,
       the fish,
       poisson,
       poison, und ob von der klinge der fischfrau skalen
sprangen, kleine, kopflose reigen oder regen, darin, wenn
man hinüberschaute, erst das glänzen, das benennen, dann
die luft verschwand.

LITTLE STAR-NOSED MOLE SPEECH

it's digging-dark in this poem, in which tongue could it pos-
sibly roam? turn on that star nose, fumble, rummage. here
a small surface, silken folds. could be diced tofu. or toffee,
if the edges were more rugged. everything rests with the
edges, but where do i rest? *lingering, not even among what's
most intimate.* long corridors, mixing of layers, well-aired, in
short: terrine. or terrier snack. if only i could get away, out-
side, where the flags of tags wave, i'd find a word for my
pretty pickle. *ah, where shall I find,* on these dark shelves of
such clean speaking, where the mead, and where the me? i
can hear coughing, a muffled trot, does he come nigh, the
dog lover? bobby-mouth? the great trekker, yes: you go
ahead and try to sell that, *lecker.*

Products that are sold in Germany must also be labeled in German.
Erika Steinbach, member of the "Verein Deutsche Sprache"

KLEINE STERNMULLREDE

sist zappenduster im gedicht, welche sprache es wohl spricht? sternnase anstellen, tasten, fahnden. schmale fläche hier, seidene falz. könnten tofuwürfel sein. oder toffee, wenn die ränder schroffer wären. an den rändern liegt so manches, nur wo lieg ich? *verweilung, auch am vertrautesten nicht.* lange gänge, mischung der schichten, luft rundum – will sagen: terrine. oder terriersnack. ach käm ich weg, nach draußen, wo die fahnen der namen wehen, ich fänd ein wort für meine lage. aber wo nehm ich, wenn in dunklen regalen, wo so ein sauberes sprechen, eigen rechts und feigen links? ich höre husten, dumpfes traben. naht er schon, der hundefreund? ein grenzermund? oder trecker, ja: verkauf die mal.

Produkte, die in Deutschland verkauft werden, müssen auch deutsch beschriftet sein.
Erika Steinbach, Mitglied im „Verein Deutsche Sprache"

MITTENS

winter came, stretched its frames,
wove misty threads into the damp

wood. fogged windows, we didn't
recognize each other by our arms

which were too big, too baggy, all
borrowed onesies, into which we would grow, if they fitted us,

which, eventually, they will. would.
a verb like the sound of sleeves over

wet glass. like wet sleeves in a mouth,
sucking. through the frames we saw

snow portraits of mothers in parks,
wind-ruffled, on the verge of, but held

by ribbons, which led to hats, in der
mitte of gloves. saw the supply-threads

of winter, linty. and tested our roles,
tentatively, along the midlines of mittens.

MITTENS

winter kam, spannte seine rahmen,
wob nebelstränge ins feuchte holz.

beschlagene fenster, wir erkannten
uns nicht an den armen, die zu groß

waren, schlackrig, geborgte strampler
allesamt, in die wir wachsen würden, wenn sie passten,

was sie dann tun. täten. ein verb wie
das geräusch von ärmeln über nasses

glas. wie nasse ärmel in einem mund,
saugend. durch die rahmen sahen wir

schneeporträts von müttern in parks,
verwehte, an den rändern, gehalten

von bändern, die zu mützen führten,
mittens. sahen die versorgungsstränge

des winters, fusselig. probten tastend
unsere rollen, an handschuhschnüren.

ON CLASSIFICATION IN LANGUAGE, A FEEBLE READER

I

the bending of our gender words began early as a set of pines near coastal dunes—lithe with level roots, androgynously grown. a settlement of expansive sight, in which we caressed, buffeted by creaky singsong of *der die das.* cassettes of our childhood! i almost said boyhood. we were more whorls than girls, you twirled me until my needles kneaded veins, compact, compass. which way did they point. pee over there, or as far as you can, truth—a high arc in this pale-hipped, scantly lifted night. never-mind verandas, moss-soft as change is. this used to be a camp for young pioneers, i said, another project to diminish differences, or to disguise them. neckerchiefs, knots, a different kind of tip-envy ruled there! my interior echo dates from this period. from this period, in our hands, all articles were political, der cup, die ladle, das beach towel, *eins, zwei, drei.* the things we hung to dry between trunks that grew askew, they always blew in line with the axis of the earth. even the wind pushed for direction, straightened them.

FIBEL MINDS
(VON DEN WORTARTEN)

I

früh begann die biegung unserer geschlechtswörter, gestaltet
als kiefern vor küstendüne – geschmeidig, mit flachen wur-
zeln, androgynem wuchs. siedlung aus weitsicht, in der
wir liebkosten, von knarzigem singsang umtost. kassetten
unserer jugend! hätte beinahe jungend gesagt. wir waren
mehr rädchen als mädchen, du drehtest an mir, bis meine
nadeln adern wurden, kompakt, kompass. wohin wiesen
die. dorthin pinkle, oder so weit, wie du kannst, wahrheit
ein hoher bogen in der hüftblassen, kurz gelüpften nacht.
egale veranden. moosweiches verändern. das war mal pio-
nierlager, sagte ich, auch so ein projekt, unterschiede zu
verkleinern, oder verkleiden. halstücher, knoten, herrschte
da ganz anderer zipfelneid! aus dieser zeit stammt mein
inneres echo. aus dieser zeit, in unseren händen, alle artikel
politisch, becher, kelle, strandhandtuch. was wir zum trock-
nen zwischen stämme hingen, die schräg wuchsen, wehte
immer erdachsengerade. selbst der wind wills von uns wis-
sen, drängt auf richtung, richtet ab.

II

dune was substantial. a thing-word or classification sport, a group of puckering hillocks. for its jutting form some called it the main fort. and yet we had seen the sea make a leap towards it, not the other way around. but sandy slopes, beige like temples. here we lay, in march, cocooned in blankets, traveling together for the first time. you'd left behind western hinterland, me: eastern, also birch trees, shivering pines through which we passed as childhood. now we sorted beach finds according to generic pleasure. some categories only contained one word: house, night, water, village, chalk. our wobbling piles, serenaded by grains of sand, which slide with them. wasn't "dune" mainly a procedure, shared knowledge, a field? it wanders, you said, as a cushion. were we still lying on it, or merely on an idea of it, which you immediately perceived to be bolder, and i to be colder? our heads poked out from under the blanket as if to say, more nameless things were puckering within.

II

düne war substanziell, dingwort oder nennsport, eine gruppe
puckernder buckel. ihre vorspringende form brachte manche
dazu, hauptort zu sagen. dabei hatten wir genau gesehen,
wie das meer einen satz auf sie zu machte, nicht umgekehrt.
aber sandgefälle, beige wie schläfen. hier lagen wir im märz,
in decken verpuppt, zum ersten mal zusammen verreist.
du hattest westliches, ich östliches hinterland gelassen, auch
birken, bibbernde kiefern, die wir als kindheit durchliefen.
jetzt sortierten wir strandfunde nach genuss. manche klas-
sen enthielten nur ein wort: haus, nacht, wasser, dorf, kalk.
wacklige stapel, von sandkörnern besungen, die gemein-
sam rutschen. hieß es nicht, düne sei vor allem prozedur,
geteiltes wissen, feld? sie wandert, sagtest du, als kissen.
lagen wir dann noch hier oder schon auf einer idee von ihr,
was dir gleich kühner vorkam, mir kühler? unsere köpfe
ragten aus der decke, als wollten sie sagen, namenlosere
dinge puckerten darin.

III

we looked for better ways to wrap what we said. we
dared go closer to the shore, burying our bodies with
our shovelling oars—water in hollows, and the knee of
the queen was chalk. we didn't know how to end this
walk. coast guards approached us, pitched adjectives as
clunky roofed beach chairs: they were supposed to ban
otherness, but our questions scattered along their walls,
marooned inside. of a groggy kind. in the march sun. which
grogged. you said: not all languages have beach chairs,
some run this thing on verbs alone. volleyball player, beach
flaneur, putting curl on it, girl you're a cut above. a certain
german poet-doctor wanted to discard all beach chairs,
something about being static. it's no skin off my nose, but
a dose of seaweed inside it i couldn't reach. it was time
to refer to papua new guinea where all things come in fives:
good, bad, big, small, other. but i didn't get round to it. the
good and small roared towards us, said boo, brought the
end of the big sentence. our mouths were full of sand, and
what we now dared ask was other, other, other, other, other,
other, other, other, other, other, other, other, other.

III

wir suchten, für was wir sagten, eine größere verpackung.
wagten uns vor zum strand, körper vergraben mit eigener
hand – wasser in kuhle, kreide ist der königin ihr knie. weiter
wussten wir nie. küstenwärter errichteten eigenschafts-
wörter, klobige körbe: sie sollten fremdheit bannen, unsere
fragen aber stoben gegen ihre wände, gekuppte hände, saßen
drin fest. mit dösiger beschaffenheit. in der märzsonne. die
döselte. du sagtest: nicht alle sprachen haben körbe, manche
ziehen das ding mit verben auf. volleyballspieler, strandspa-
zierer, rädchen lauf, mädchen mach was her. und ein dich-
terdoktor wollte alle strandkörbe streichen, irgendwas mit
deren statik. mich juckte das gar nicht, dafür ein tangstrick
an der nase, ich kam nicht ran. es war zeit, auf papua-neu-
guinea zu verweisen, wo alle dinge wirklich fünf sind: gut,
schlecht, groß, klein, anders. ich kam nicht dazu. das gute
mehr brauste ran, machte buh, brachte ende vom großen
satz. wir hatten mund voll sand, und was wir jetzt zu fragen
wagten, war anders, anders, anders, anders, anders, anders,
anders, anders, anders, anders, anders, anders, anders.

II.

Subsisters

All subtitles invariably transform the original text. …
Transformative subtitling implies that the original is not
only what it is, but that it also exceeds itself.
Eric Cazdyn, "A New Line in the Geometry"

35

I

original version

lauren's youngest sister has a gift for already leading guests on in the vestibule. casually, the way she—when he still stands—floats onto his lap: only with words. after all we live in the foyer, no one's obliged. antics, acrobatics, to be a nice mantle—everything's camouflage. while lauren warms the marble statue by the staircase, i work out our tactics: resemblance. that way everyone sees us, and no one can take what isn't ours.

lauren's youngest sister has a gift for leading guests steadily out of the vestibule. wordily, casually, sir has hardly turned the key, he's already floating out. we just live differently in the foyer, not obliged to our own. we could do worse than wear mantelpieces, a marble statue warms you better than your own thin skin. it'd be the one to resemble us: the worse for wear, maybe ours after all.

i mean, men sind nur big sleepers, right. das einzige what makes them blink is mink.

english version

young sister lauren has a gift for guests, a gift for pleading, for her guests' vests, casually, weigh wordy, casual, sir, barely turns the key, it's already floating out. we live for yer, no abloquation on our own. antiques, apropos tics, to be a marble statue warns you better than your own thin spin. taken that, perhaps we'd still see *was*: she'd be the one to assemble us. the verse to wear, maybe hours after ohr.

I

OV

laurens jüngste schwester hat die gabe, gäste schon im vesti-
bül zu verführen. sportlich, wie sie, wenn der herr noch
steht, bereits auf seinen schoß schwebt: nur mit worten. wir
leben ja in der eingangshalle, man ist zu nichts verpflichtet.
anstand, handstand, ein schöner mantel sein – tarnung ist
alles. während lauren die marmorstatue an der treppe wärmt,
kläre ich unsere taktik: ähnlichkeit. so kann uns jeder sehen,
und keiner nehmen, was uns nicht gehört.

OmU

laurens jüngste schwester hat die gabe, gäste schonend aus dem vestibül zu führen. wortgewandt, sportlich, kaum dreht der herr am schloss, da schwebt er schon hinaus. wir leben eben anders in der eingangshalle, unserem nichts verpflichtet. wir richten weniger als schöne mäntel an, man wärmt sich besser mit der marmorstatue als mit unserer dünnen haut. die sieht uns immerhin ähnlich: etwas mitgenommen, vielleicht gehört sie uns auch.

i mean, men are just big sleepers, right. the only thing that makes them blink is mink.

II

barbara's back. hooked, lined, and cooked. no one talked faster, ran farther, never far enough. i'm helping her unpack her suitcase: gooseflesh, when the slip-dress-silk ripples through my fingers, and on her gown the sparkle of sequins … keep it. barbara badgers. in every corner of the room she lights another cigarette. outside the window lies lackluster the little-town-dusk, the damn clapping sea, night of little fishes.

barbara's back. booked, signed, and blasé. sharp gasp, another take cut fair enough. i'm helping her unpack her suitcase: all flesh and fingers, the silk slips like water, and with the gown the sequence … barbara's badge sparkles it. in each, she says, there's another room with corners, cigarette, threaded borders, and outside again: a window, tiny town, a dam, a little sea, applauding the fishes all night.

      meine schwester hasst fische. they don't talk much, and their scales make such tacky dresses.

english version

barbara is backed. both fort and da, that's the catch, in the breath. fast schnapp for air, another run-through, far far enough. i help. pack your things, skins, silks: all film and finger, she streams through my hands, with paillettes and little fishes. blink blink, barbara's *keck* whinge, she sequins, another fag, another fad, pacing the room, cornered, like fish, nightly applauded, in a window of sea.

II

OV

barbara ist zurück. hooked, caught and cooked. keine konnte schneller sprechen, weiter laufen, nie weit genug. ich helfe ihr, den koffer auszupacken. gänsehaut, wenn mir die slip-dress-seide durch die finger rinnt, und auf dem abendkleid das glänzen der pailletten ... kannste haben. barbara keckert. in jeder zimmerecke steckt sie eine neue zigarette an. vorm fenster fad die dämmerung der kleinen stadt, das kleine klatschende meer, nacht der kleinen fische.

OmU

barbara ist zurück. fortgegangen, hergefangen. schnelles
schnappen, weiterer durchlauf, nicht weit genug. ich helfe
ihr, den koffer auszupacken: ganz haut und hand, die seide
liegt wie wasser an, und mit dem abendkleid ... die die pail-
letten ... kannste glänzen. barbara keckert. in jeder, sagt sie,
steckt ein neues zimmer, immer mit ecke, zigarette, fäden,
dahinter wieder fenster, winzig eine stadt, ein damm, ein
kleines meer, das nachts den kleinen fischen applaudiert.

**my sister hates fish. they don't talk much, and
their scales make such tacky dresses.**

III

original version

jane, who could be my aunt, and i shared joys and sorrows in the club. i say tree nursery, jane: beehive. apart from that: no agreement. but the garden, the gardener, the sycamore's glowing red and the rosebush too, by the house. i encourage her: do anything. by the setting sun she's still a stunner. that headscarf works for her, and in her sunglasses, when saying goodbye, the rows of houses on the street flow back into their ornamental shades.

jane, for my aunts, always meant joy. her sorrows layered into the colors baumschule and bienenstock. my agreement with jane was the garden where we housed the gärtner, the glowing wood of sycamore in ambush: jane had courage, she buried it all on her own. never out of her depths, she lifts, with the setting sun, her stunned gaze, or what remains of it, under a headscarf. in her shades, the street houses ornaments, rows of them, flowing.

my sister was too old for the nursery. but the gardener wasn't old enough.

bienenstock, gehstock, nursed into walking and variant blushes. agreed, the gardener meant maple, red, and glowing: jane, anything you like, very much, cheer cheer, brazenly so. dig deeper. say goodbye. look what remains of it, stunned by the sun am busch, by edging depths, flowing houses, glasses, film up, and our goodbyes work their way back into our ornaments.

III

OV

mit jane, sie könnte meine tante sein, freud und leid im club geteilt. ich sage baumschule, jane beehive. sonst kaum über-einstimmungen. aber der garten, der gärtner, das glühende rot des ahorns und der rosenstock am haus: ich ermutige jane zu allem. im grunde ist sie, gegen die untergehende sonne, noch immer ein hingucker. ihr kopftuch arbeitet für sie, in der sonnenbrille, beim abschied, fließen die häuser der straße zurück in ihre zierfarben.

mit jane verbanden meine tanten immer freud. ihr leiden
unterteilt in die farben baumschule und beehive. meine
vereinbarung mit jane war der garten, darin wir die gardner,
das glühende holz des ahorns und den roten gehstock unter-
brachten: jane war so mutig, alles allein zu vergraben. aus
dieser tiefe hebt sie, mit untergehender sonne, den blick, was
davon bleibt, unterm kopftuch. in den gläsern arbeitet die
straße sich in ihre zierhäuser vor.

**my sister was too old for the nursery, but the
gardener wasn't old enough.**

IV

when tallulah turns her famous cartwheel, the party's delighted. they all whisper and kiss, we didn't even miss tallulah's underwear! that i wear it, no one knows. we call the ballroom 'lifeboat,' bathed in blue silk, and when tallu-lah calls me by her sister's name, who's simply "sister," i fol-low her aboard. that way she keeps every secret in the open. until the break of day, we share a warm vest, unrecognized, and the wind.

original version with subtitles

if you talk to tallulah about being famous, it turns into a party. kissing delighted, underway whispering, a harbour for everything you'd otherwise miss. where, we don't know for the life of us. but if the ballroom's a boat of blue silk that sinks with us, every dance is a distress call to a stranger sister, simply "schwester." das will tallulah. she takes me, like an open secret, on board, and keeps it. make or break, sure, i'm part warm vest, part wind, unreconciled.

       so dreht sie sich inside out. was wie ein lifeboat scheint ist in fact der ozean.

english version

ask tallulah, they all whisper, we missed a kiss that no one knows it's wearing. ich trage sie, my lingerie as life vest, call me sister, alle an bord, tallulah's adored, by the party, the delight, the hushed somersaults. if you ask me for advice, when she ahoys me, my distress unwinds, in the morning, the blue-silked call, the waltzing secret, takes me for buoyancy, for sisterly secrets uncloaked, and the warm mink sinks with me.

IV

als tallulah ihr berühmtes rad schlägt, ist die party entzückt.
alle küssen sich, flüstern, sie hätten tallulahs unterwäsche
überhaupt nicht vermisst. dass ich sie trage, weiß ja keiner.
den tanzsaal nennen wir ein rettungsboot, umspült von
blauer seide, und wenn tallulah mich ruft, beim namen ihrer
schwester, die einfach sister heißt, folg ich ihr an bord. so
bewahrt sie jedes geheimnis durch enthüllung. wir teilen bis
zum morgen eine warme weste, unerkannt, den wind.

OmU

wenn man tallulah um rat fragt, schlägt sie eine party vor. dazu entzücktes küssen, flüstern, ein unterschlupf für alles, was man sonst vermisst. ob es trägt, wissen wir nicht. doch wenn der saal ein schiff aus blauer seide ist, das mit uns untergeht, wird jeder tanz zum rettungsruf, gesandt an eine unbekannte schwester, schlicht sister. so will es tallulah. sie nimmt mich, wie ein offenes geheimnis, an bord, behält es. teils bin ich eine warme weste, teils am morgen der wind.

so she turns herself inside out. what seems to be a lifeboat is in fact the ocean.

V

original version

who sent marlene those dolls? they sit on the deserted dress-
ing table, nipping champagne. dolls, tell me your names, top
hat perhaps, or powder box? the sloppy mouths keep silent.
through the trellis light threads off-kilter strings, draws
stars into the wall, into this heat. the doll with the darker
skin murmurs: marlene is a ventriloquist now. another sings
a song: there once was a tailcoat that later turned to dust,
and our nieces, too, began to rust, marie, malade, madame.

they sent marlene into the desert on a dolly. whoever nips champagne at her table, dressed only in a top and a hat, pulls the strings; they say she's like a powdery cloud mouthed into allusive silence. the light filters through the slanted window—it's too hot, we understand, to be a star. suddenly she raises her voice, without a body, to a song, a rumoring dark tailcoat vents drolly another sin, dusting the niches, where our missus is a mirage, mal d'art.

my sister left to become a star. people say she deserted us, but i know better …

english version

marlene packs the wild dolls for her dessert of champagne and silence. tipped hat, this table cylinders out of control. say, is this a mouth pursing lips, a slanted widow, those light shawls heat every star well, for running threads. the mirage suits the doll who sings a song, *toll!* suddenly praises her choices, those bodies in trellis, tailed and coated, ein rumoren from the venting crowds, her entourage, vielleicht morgen, mal d'aubade, how *schade*.

V

OV

wer hat marlene die puppen geschickt? sie sitzen auf dem
wüsten schminktisch, nippen am champagner. könnt ihr
mir sagen, wie ihr heißt, zylinder etwa, puderfass? die nas-
sen münder schweigen. durchs fenstergitter fällt in schrägen
fäden licht, zeichnet in der hitze sterne an die wand. marlene
ist jetzt bauchrednerin, raunt da die puppe mit der dunklen
haut. die andere singt ein lied. war einst ein frack, war später
staub, und unsere nichten auch, marie, malade, madame.

OmU

man schickte marlene zum verpuppen in die wüste. wer
hier an ihrem schminktisch am champagner nippt, der hat
die fäden in der hand. man sagt, sie sei wie eine puderwolke
im zylinder, schweigsam, schwer zu fassen. durchs schräge
fenster streicht das licht, es ist zu heiß, verstehen wir, um
zu gefallen. da hebt sich plötzlich ihre stimme, ohne leib,
zu einem lied, ein summend dunkler frack, morgana, leicht
malade, dann staub, dann lange nichts.

**my sister left to become a star. people say she
deserted us, but i know better ...**

VI

with aunt lana at the petrol station, at the beach, the theater. a day like a script. we're in her dressing room before the window-sized mirror, her game's mine, meins, quite simply, goof. on her cabinet a patch of ash, the *drama review*, the letter just penned, to detlef, as i know. but i don't know where the light comes from. in the golden frame behind her the room is running late into darkness, delays itself into the dark. under these circumstances i don't find myself rendered completely, not quite on call.

original version with subtitles

stationed with aunt lana in the theater patrol. the script says beach. we practice, fronting the window-sized mirrors, she's a play-mine, i'm all dimples, aloof. we patch the *escritoire* **with ash, the** *drama review***, the white in the letter to detlef too. if there shall be light again who knows, and yet in the golden range of frames she holds up, dark and late. those circumstantial selves, as usual, render me an unfinished encore.**

really, my mom's sister is an imitation of herself. she smokes and the mirror lights up.

english version

aunt lana's tank top says a day at the beach *is* **a script. i patrol her theatrically. we practice. we play mirrors, size each other up, quite gemein, dim down, the ash's proof. with esprit and cash we write, the drama, the letters, lightly and knowing. a stain. if, again, and yet. our extent is dark, as usual, we're framed into golden latitudes, for good measure, not quite da capo.**

VI

OV

mit tante lana an der tanke, am strand, im theater. ein tag wie
ein script. jetzt sitzen wir in ihrer garderobe vor dem fenster-
großen spiegel, ihr spiel mine, meines, wie üblich, murks. auf
dem toilettentisch ein aschefleck, die nachtkritik, der ange-
fangene brief, an detlef, wie ich weiß. woher das licht kommt,
weiß ich nicht. im goldenen rahmen hinter ihr verspätet sich
der raum ins dunkel. unter diesen umständen finde ich nur
mich nicht ganz wiedergegeben.

OmU

mit tante lana zum auftanken ins theater. im script steht
strand. jetzt üben wir vor fenstergroßen spiegeln, sie spiel-
grube, ich grübchen, hinter uns murks. tücher markieren wir
mit asche, die nachtkritik, das weiß im angefangenen brief
an detlef auch. ob noch mal licht kommt, weiß ich nicht,
und doch im goldenen bereich der rahmen hält sie, dunkel
und spät. die umstehenden nehmen mich wie üblich nur als
halbe zugabe wahr.

**really, my mom's sister is an imitation of herself.
she smokes, and the mirror lights up.**

VII

gene's a genie, bashful. i want to paint her portrait, but she doesn't stay still. her coat is white, her hat is white, and then the quiet, gray flicker of the fireplace—it's hard to find her contours. a shadow's cast on the fauteuil. he shows us his credentials. gene and i don't waver, we leave the canvas, which we call laura, to him, and run past his immobile face, the old grandfather clock and the testimony of the false interior.

gene's a genius, embarrassed by her genes. neither she nor i can picture that. a white coat, that yes, fires the pace a whit, we quiet the hot bickering, not hard to call it borderline. not even the color of the armchair lends us credence. released from the canvassed witness, the aura of a false name, gene and i wager that our interior shadow will pass, we clock him, steadfast, granted there's no further fuss.

       electroshock? sister, being in the picture doesn't mean you have to play a painting.

english version
some gin for gene, *gerne*, no shame. thou shalt not make an image of a coat. at a standstill it is white, a blank face, those why's, we place the fire into wit, the sketchy glint of it. not even the armchair could be duller. it bends to our confidentials. gene and i grant laura leave, call it her fault, and run into the canvas, that graver silhouette, and when we can't go further, we test the ledge's steadiness with our *fuß*.

VII

gene geniert sich. ich will ein bild von ihr malen, aber sie hält
nicht still. ihr mantel ist weiß, ihr hut ist weiß, dazu das leise,
graue flackern im kamin – es ist schwer, hier ihre grenze
zu finden. ein schatten liegt auf dem fauteuil. er zeigt uns
seinen ausweis. wir lassen ihm die leinwand, die wir laura
nennen, und rennen, gene und ich, vorbei an seinem unbe-
weglichen gesicht, der alten standuhr und der zeugenschaft
des falschen interieurs.

OmU

wer schämt sich nicht manchmal seiner gene. weder sie noch
ich haben ein bild davon. ein weißer mantel, das schon, aber
was weiß der hut, das graue flackern im kamin – klarer fall
von borderline. nicht einmal die farbe des lehnsessels weist
uns aus. entlassen sind wir aus der zeugenschaft des segel-
tuchs, der aura eines falschen namens, gene und ich, und
schließen wetten ab, dass unsere einrichtung vorübergeht,
mit starre, standuhr, licht, gesicht.

**electroshocks? sister, being in the picture
doesn't mean you have to play a painting.**

III.

Method Acting with Anna O.

In the early 1880s, having nursed her sick father, a young Viennese woman named Bertha Pappenheim found herself being treated by Dr Joseph Breuer for seeing and hearing impairments, signs of paralysis, anxiety, and hallucinations. The doctor diagnosed hysteria. During her treatment under hypnosis, Anna O. (as the patient was later called in Freud's and Breuer's "Studies on Hysteria" in 1895) referred to her treatment as the "talking cure" or "chimney sweeping"—rattling off stories in free association. This later contributed to the myth of Anna O. as the founder of psychoanalysis. Her symptoms comprised, among others, the rejection of certain foods, prosopagnosia (face blindness), as well as loss of linguistic coherence—at times she could only speak and understand English. After breaking off the treatment and after her move to Frankfurt, Bertha Pappenheim became a committed social worker and women's rights activist who fought and campaigned against prostitution and the international trafficking in Jewish women. On her many socio-politically motivated travels she also collected samples of rare lace. Her collection is held in the Museum of Applied Arts in Vienna.

65

Annalogues
Annaloge

ANNALOGUE ON ORANGES

when it is time for oranges, ist keine zeit, no time at all,
für nichts. i only eat oranges, at least they exist, even if not
much else is, no things at all, not much. petite little boats
and stringy thin skin! i suck on them for hours. keeps me
busy. free run for the tongue, looking for thread between
teeth, interlace-space, and rooms to own, not much.
oranges or existence all round. oranges or residence all
round. with weighty curtains and rooms that step together
conspiring, brother, mother, doctor, and the wardress, daily
a session, that's how they planned it all, wall to wall around
my standstill arms. but oranges exist, as transportation,
outside my window, orange busses, orange trains, over
cobbled headstone pavement, rattling through the ages.
and on my bed those glimmering signals—peel, swinging
segments, white skinned bridges! i lay them out for hours.
keeps me going drüber. while the wardress brings fresh
water fresh sheets, all the unemptied glasses, cups. daily a
warding off for repair, nicht wahr, that's how they planned
it all. later ten rooms on each floor, servants galore, with
bow and tie marriage and tea. marriage and in the eve-
ning a little riot, then tea. but when it is time for oranges,
ist keine zeit, no time at all for thirst, für wasser, for being
thus arranged. because oranges are their own maneuver-
ing material. because trains, bridges, and little glimmer-
ing glitches keep me going unallayed. go lack go lack use
to her. because oranges communicate through the ages.
oranges or restricted residence all round. oranges or a
rather limited range of vision. oranges or it's like we're in
prison. just trees and animals, we're at the Ende der Welt.
when it is time for oranges, ist keine zeit, no time at all, for
world-endings, padlock-curtains, paper measures for sure.
because oranges are center-residence for life. for a lack, for
want, go go be good, of use to her. go sweep the chimney,
so that the doctor comes again. that the doctor sees how
organs wander. through the ages. that's what they figured:
that they wander and then go astray. get stuck in the body,
block vocal tracts, good manner tracts. o range of things.
because storage, and organs, organs. because collect your-
self, then wander. glimmering bright and lacking. against

I, a native something-or-other-girl

"solide

"geistige Nahrung   and she digested

mit affektiver athletik

und orangenpoetiqqqqq

or as you say   ein organ haben

"Starting from or with an orange, all travels are possible.
All ways of the voice that lead across it, are good."

or as you say   eine parole haben :

you tell me what it means

or french   a lengevitch on parole

(dry up in mid-speech

stuck : repeat :

a)   ich have krämpfe in my calves
b)   my teeth klappern

orderly arrangements. against measures, wall to wall, around my standstill warning. only at first did i snap off buttons from covers and cases. then dropped my cover, coherence, a show at tick and loosen loosen it so to speak, sat. wanted to, the cover, come out from under, come out loose, what they call paralysis, i call a tick. a ticking in oranges, through the ages. because i can hear it. where i sit, in my barracks in the forest, my vienna asylum, my tent on the rindermarkt. where i suck it out, for hours, what's lacking. let the tongue run free, looking for grounds between teeth, rejection, residence, waiting rooms. keeps me beschäftigt. because i not having work, no travel only thought-revel, thought-cuttings. while the wardress takes away the peel, their sauer glimmer all over my lack of thirst. nein, i did not pretend. hungerstreik. because oranges are asylum and solid geistig nourishment. glimmering. because one ought to freely choose what one eats, right, packages, laced with marriage, biscuits and tea. haven't you the faintest, and of that a great deal, when nothing else appeals, no things at all, nicht viel. but brothers and dogs, they too exist, if you can stomach it, as is the custom as many things are. stutter-juice and whoops! open the sluice! when it is time for oranges, ist keine zeit, no time at all, for brothers, who go off to study, or dogs on all fours, mind you, slobbering all over my tray, drinking out of my little cup. naughty pup! oh long black tongue. why ich this knows. sniffing outside, du hund du. snap drank sloppily from the little cup, with the dog-tongue, the same indeed freilich thinks often to tame it—dors dors! must i be sick and therefore break? ah no alors! break only rules about drinking, non, only tea-duties and ten-room ditties, marriage, trays, parentage, offspring, and tea. nein, ich have not this thirst, never, nie. that's what they figured, right, that even a dog has more rights to run free. but that oranges glimmer. that one can with an orange an existence derange and switch track. so as not to be slurped up by dog-tongue. by forest-fence. instead usurp, heavy curtains, paper measures. excuse-moi, dog. excuse-moi, docteur. can he not betake himself away? and take the warding off, the water, the cups and every wall they mounted round my little bed. you see, oranges solidarize, those round sashaying organs, i join their wanderings. i squeeze and out comes contra-stand:
orange in. orange in.

I, a native irgendwas girl

1 2 3 4 5

NO YES, namely_____german_____

but I will try to give, as well, as a person

between 9 o'clock in the evening

till I p. mn.*

"absences, which I could observe myself

by a strange feeling of 'timemissing'"

but I will try to give, as well, as a person

"a windfall

when I was circling round the oranges"

island, camp, a glimmer, a glimpse

"When I was circling round the oranges, who paid then?
Who wrote then?"

wenn es zeit ist für orangen, ist keine zeit, no time at all, für nichts. ich esse nur orangen, at least they exist, wenn sonst nicht viel ist, no things at all, nicht viel. zierliche schiffchen und zähe dünne haut! ich zutsche sie stundenlang aus. keeps me beschäftigt. der zunge ihren auslauf, sucht nach fäden zwischen zähnen, spitzenräume, zimmeretage, nicht viel. orangen oder rundum existenz. orangen oder rundum residenz. mit gewichtigen vorhängen, zimmern, die zusammentreten, bruder, mutter, doktor, wärterin, täglich eine tagung, so hatten sies gedacht, wand für wand um meine lahm gelegten arme. doch orangen existieren, transportmittel, orange busse, orange züge, kopfsteinpflaster vor dem fenster, rattern durch die zeiten. und auf dem bett leuchtende zeichen – schalen, schaukelstücke, weiß wattierte brücken! ich lege sie stundenlang aus. keeps me going drüber. während wärterin mit wasser kommt, mit frischen bettbezügen, all die nicht geleerten gläser, tassen. täglich eine wartung, nicht wahr, so hatten sies gedacht, dann mehrzimmeretage, eignes personal, ehe und tee. ehe und am abend kleine rage, dann tee. aber wenn es zeit ist für orangen, ist es keine zeit, no time at all für durst, für wasser, für sich arrangieren lassen. weil orangen sind ihr eignes rangiermaterial. weil züge, brücken und schiffchen, keeps me going unbeschwichtigt. go lack go lack use to her. weil orangen kommunizieren, durch die zeiten. orangen oder rundum residenzpflicht. orangen oder rundum eine grenzsicht. it's like we're in prison. just trees and animals, we're at the end of the world. wenn es zeit ist für orangen, ist es keine zeit, not time at all, für weltenden, schlossvorhänge, papiervorgänge. weil orangen sind lebensmittelpunkt. weil ein mangel, mangel, geh sei ihr von nutzen. geh die esse putzen, dass der doktor wiederkommt. dass der doktor sieht, wie die orangen wandern. durch die zeiten. nicht wahr, so hatten sies gedacht: wandern und kommen vom weg ab. bleiben stecken im körper, stimmwege verstopft, benimmwege. o range of things. weil storage, und organs, organs. weil sich sammeln, dann wandern. leuchtende und lacking. gegen die ordnungen. gegen verordnungen, wand für wand, um meine lahm gelegte warnung. ich hab nur anfangs knöpfe abgerissen von bezügen. dann die

I, a native irgendwas girl

„solide

„geistige Nahrung   und sie verdaute

            mit affektiver athletik

                                            und

orangenpoetiqqqqq

oder wie man sagt   ein organ haben

„Ausgehend von der Orange sind alle Reisen möglich.
Alle Stimmwege, die über sie führen, sind gut.“

oder wie man sagt   eine parole haben

            im sinne von englisch freigang

                                oder french

freisprechanlage

(mitten im sprechen stecken

            bleiben : wiederholen :

bezüge gelassen, wo sie sind. a show at tick and loosen loosen it so to speak sat. hab mich lösen von bezügen, sie nennen es lähmung, ich nenne es tick. ein ticken in orangen, durch die zeiten. weil ich es höre. wo ich sitze, in meiner waldbaracke, meiner wienklatsche, meinem zelt auf dem rindermarkt. wo ich zutsche, stundenlang, was fehlt. der zunge ihren auslauf, sucht nach gründen zwischen zähnen, auflassräume, aufenthalte. keeps me beschäftigt. weil ich keine arbeit haben. keine reisen, nur gedankenschneisen. während wärterin die schalen wegnimmt, ihr saures glimmern über meinen keinen durst. nein, ich hab das nicht gespielt. hungerstreik. weil orangen asyl und solide geistige nahrung. leuchten. weil man aussuchen dürfen muss, was man isst, oder nicht, pakete, geschnürt mit ehe, keks und tee. davon eine ahnung, wenn sonst nicht viel ist, no things at all, nicht viel. aber brüder und hunde, die gibt es auch. das ist hier bauch. stottersaft und hoppla, schleusen aufgemacht! wenn es zeit ist für orangen, ist es keine zeit, no time at all, für brüder, die studieren, oder hunde, die auf allen vieren. mind you. machen sich über mein tablett. trinken gar aus meinem becherchen. frecherchen! oh long black tongue. woher ich das knows. draußen schnuppern, dog you dog. schnapp hat schlabbrig aus dem becher getrunken, mit der hundezunge, derselbe glaubt nämlich häufig, sie beherrschen zu dürfen – dors, dors! muss ich jetzt brechen, non, nur die regel von trinken und essen, non, nur teepflicht und vermehrte zimmer. ehe, tabletten, herkunft und tee. nein, ich habe nicht diesen durst. so hatten sies gedacht, nicht wahr, dass selbst ein hund mehr recht auf seinen freigang hat. aber dass orangen leuchten. dass man mit orangen kann eine existenz rangieren aus. statt wegzuschlecken lassen sich von hundezunge. von zaun im wald. wegstecken, schwere vorhänge, papiervorgänge. excuse-moi, dog. excuse-moi, doktor. steht immerhin vor dem zelt. was hier schickt sich nicht. was, schickt er sich nicht selber fort? und nimmt die wartung mit, wasser, rahmen, planen, jede wand, die man um mich gestellt. weil orangen solidarisieren, runde flutschende organe, schließ mich ihrem wandern an. weil squeeze und raus ein widerstand:

orange in. orange in.

a) i have cramps in my calves

b) my teeth chatter

I, a native something girl

1 2 3 4 5

NO YES, namely_____german_____

but will try to give, as well, as a person

between 9 o'clock in the evening

till I p. mn.*

„als ich um die Orange kreiste, wer zahlte da? Wer schrieb da?"

abwesenheiten, die ich selbst durch ein merkwürdiges
gefühl von "beobachten können (time missing)"

but will try to give, as well, as a person

„einen Glücksfall

als ich um die Orange kreiste"

Insel, Camp, ein Leuchten

oh such recognizing work. they say surplus, i say bloody overplus, blossom guff. they ruffle and puff up pillows, i hiss: what can all this green stuff be? a face is what one goes by, generally. or was i a plant sans licht left in the basement. i do not mean this literally. later i do. jaffa, haifa, alexandria. such recognizing work. they say father still, I say familiar skull—although I haven't seen him in a while. they keep me away as it exerts me so. around my bed they line up people and I don't know who they are, arrange eyes left and right of a nose, in the middle below it a mouth, a dernier cri but worn. hallo, have we not met before? one side of what. the other side of what. only der doktor, ah der doktor, what a beard can, dance around the face, serving recognition, fine. dancerbeard on duty again. i do not mean this officiously. later i do. jaffa, haifa, alexandria. such rec-ognizing work. again der doktor fluffs up pillows, brings me a bunch, and so it comes to light: i suffer floral tunnel vision. je dis: une fleur! je dis: une fleur! what grand mal-heur. eyes see room, taffeta-curtains, pile-up of bourgeois gushes, just the very bouquets i can't get a handle on, only single blossoms, suspended. later kurt schwitters got it, der doktor, with his jitter, scents it not. they: a rather limited range of vision. i: anna-blume-talent! they leave the room, disintegrated by my forgetfulness. and yet i only see blank. i am only an apprentice still. that one, to make an image, must disregard arrangements. one side of what. the other side of what. lemberg, tarnopol, stanislau. plant, and two years sans licht. i pick at things until they look bigger or smaller than they were. until what's far sounds near, what's near so far. hallo, have we not before. until the doors open and one casts one's kin adrift. out onto the streets. they say: a family is what one goes by, generally. kairo, haifa, alex-andria. all the girls and sticky promises, marriage tickets, divorce letters. *so eine stolze menschenblüte in solcher umge-bung zu solchem lebenszweck geboren.* they say: and another committee, i say: pffft seriously. and they clear the room, disintegrated by my relentlessness. and yet i do not feel krank! unchaperoned, although it doesn't look nice. until the doors open and out onto the streets. i do not mean this oder was the thimble tells

     i dislike that phase that i was made to wear

     ich sagte

Alice! I don't know :

das principle case is called face blindness

"Je ne dirai a personne que mon père n'est pas mort.
C'est une de ces vérités pour lesquelle je n'ai pas encore
de mots."

that a promise?   ich erinner

     oder

a fan!   mich nicht

     oder

a fleur!   have we not before?

     the answer a grin in the tree: drive that fact home

Alice! das principle case is called

     a few ~~bilingual~~ inscriptions
     bifloral

locally. elsewhere i do. they say: ten things changed in the mirror room. i say: ten faces you'll erinner soon. i know they are changing things. i know father died though they didn't say. why else would i wear socks in the coffer of the night. always dressed, when the lid opens, when a skull's face, black snakes dance. nur der vater, ah der vater, what a skull can, cancels the face, serving recognition, fine. i do not mean this wearily. later i do. i wasn't there when father died. i do not know how a face is read. someone enters, has the nose like this, the hair like that, the wardress certainly, mother, stand and unfold yourself! and yet i only speak frank. unchaperoned, although it wouldn't look nice. jaffa, kairo, alexandria. i say: doktor, one doesn't need an image of the face. only single noses, floating eyes, also grinning, just a background. waxworks. beard crumbs. nein, even that isn't enough. i demand equal rights for flowers! for animals. face blindness for talg und klaviere! and the girls in tarnopol, konstantinopel, stanislau. oh such recognizing work. locked up until homesick wears off. until language evaporates left and right off the nose. i pluck at conditions until they look bigger or smaller than they were. a tiresome business, hatching. barely flourished, zero recogniziert. they say a flower is what one goes by, generally. when trading florists, flower smugglers draw their dark paths through europe. they say: we make a business with such bodies, with blossoms, poesie. and i say: we will see. what can all the green stuff be?

but will try to give, as well, as a person

the extent to which the symptom

or experience applies to you :

"people and things look bigger than usual"

"i see things around me differently than usual (for example, as if looking through a tunnel, or merely seeing part of an object)"

I have bin told
There was a ~~boy~~
~~There was a boy~~

i mean i dislike that fate that i was made to where

oh such recognizing work. sie sagen überschuss, ich sage
bluterguss, blütenstuss. sie fluffen kissen auf, ich hisse: what
can all that green stuff be? a face is what one goes by, gen-
erally. oder war ich eine pflanze und im keller ohne licht.
ich meine das nicht wörtlich. später schon. jaffa, haifa,
alexandria. such recognizing work. sie sagen vater noch, ich
sage totenkopf – obwohl, ich hab ihn lange nicht gesehen.
sie halten mich fern, weil es mich anstrengt. sie stellen per-
sonen ums bett, die ich nicht kenne, arrangieren augen links
und rechts von einer nase, in der mitte drunter mund, ge-
tragen nach gar keinem letzten schrei. hallo, haben wir uns
nicht schon mal? one side of what. the other side of what.
nur der doktor, ah der doktor, was ein bart kann, tänzelt ums
gesicht, erkennungsdienstlich. dancerbeard im dienst again.
ich meine das nicht behördlich. später schon. jaffa, haifa,
alexandria. such recognizing work. wieder flufft der doktor
kissen auf, er zeigt mir einen blumenstrauß, so kommt es
endlich raus: ich habe den floralen tunnelblick. je dis: une
fleur! je dis: une fleur! was grand malheur. augen sehen zim-
mer, taftvorhänge, aufstau bürgerlicher fluten, bloß sträuße
krieg ich nicht in blick, nur einzeln schwebende blüten.
später verstand das kurt schwitters, der doktor nichts gewit-
tert. sie: gesichtsfeldeinengung! ich: annablumetalent! und
verlassen das zimmer, aufgelöst von meiner vergesslich-
keit. dabei geh ich nur in die lehre. dass man, um ein bild
zu machen, von gebinden absehen muss. one side of what.
the other side of what. lemberg, tarnopol, stanislau. pflanze,
und zwei jahre nicht am licht. ich zupfe so lange an dingen,
bis sie größer oder kleiner aussehen als gehabt. bis, was fern
ist, nah klingt, nahes fern. hallo, haben wir uns nicht. bis die
türen aufgehen und man seine sippe auf die straße setzt. sie
sagen: a family is what one goes by, generally. kairo, haifa,
alexandria. all die mädchen und die klebrigen versprechen,
heiratsscheine, scheidungsbriefe. so eine stolze menschen-
blüte in solcher umgebung zu solchem lebenszweck geboren.
sie sagen: noch ein komitee, ich sage: na gehts noch. und
räumen das zimmer, aufgelöst von meiner unnachgiebigkeit.
dabei gebe ich nur in die leere. unbegleitet, although it
doesn't look nice. bis die türen aufgehen und man seine sitte
auf die straße. ich meine das nicht örtlich. anderswo schon.

oder was der fingerhut erzählt

i dislike that phase that i was made to wear

ich sagte

Alice! I don't know :

das principle fach heißt face blindness

„Ereignisse dieser Art werden oft vergessen, vor allem dann,
wenn kurze Zeit später das vorzeitige Ableben des betreffenden
Vaters auf sie folgt."

ob das ein versprechen   ich erinnere

   oder

ein fächer!   mich nicht

   oder

ein fleur!   haben wir uns schon mal?

    antwort ein grinsen im baum: drive that fact home

Alice! das principle fach heißt

a few ~~bilingual~~ inscriptions
blumige

sie sagen: zehn dinge, die im zimmer verändert. ich sage:
zehn gesichter, who you remember. ich weiß, dass sie sachen
verändern. ich weiß, dass der vater starb, sie haben es mir
nicht gesagt. warum sonst trag ich socken im koffer der
nacht. immer angezogen, wenn der deckel aufgeht, wenn ein
totenkopfgesicht, schwarze schlangen tanzen. nur der vater,
ah der vater, was ein totenkopf kann, cancelt das gesicht,
erkennungsdienstlich. ich meine das nicht beschwerlich.
später schon. ich war nicht da, als der vater starb. ich weiß
nicht, wie man liest ein gesicht. jemand tritt auf, hat nase
so, haare so, kann nur sein die wärterin, die mutter, stand
and unfold yourself! dabei ging ich in die leere. unbegleitet,
although it wouldn't look nice. jaffa, kairo, alexandria. ich
sage: doktor, man braucht kein bild vom gesicht. nur nase
einzeln, augen schweben rum, auch grinsen, bloß ein hinter-
grund. wachsfiguren. am bart die krumen. nein, selbst das ist
nicht genug. ich fordere gleiches recht für blumen! für tiere.
gesichtsblindheit für talg und klaviere! und für die mädchen
in tarnopol, konstantinopel, stanislau. oh such recognizing
work. eingesperrt, bis das heimweh verflogen. bis die sprache
verflogen, links und rechts der nase. ich rupfe so lange an
zuständen, bis sie näher oder ferner aussehen als gehabt. ein
mühsames geschäft, brüten. kaum floriert, null recogniziert.
they say a flower is what one goes by, generally. wenn blu-
menhändler, blumenschmuggler ihre dunklen wege durch
europa ziehen. sie sagen: we make a business with such bod-
ies, with blüten, poesie. und ich sage: we will see. what can
all the green stuff be?

but will try to give, as well, as a person

the extent to which

the symptom

or experience applies

to you :

„people and things look bigger than usual"

„I see things around me differently than usual (for example, as
if looking through a tunnel, or merely seeing part of an object)"

I have bin told
There was a ~~boy~~
~~There was a boy~~

i mean dislike that fate that i was made to where

Deutsch

Tatting

We have nothing new to say on the question of the origin of these dispositional hypnoid states. They often, it would seem, grow out of the day-dreams which are so common even in healthy people and to which needlework and similar occupations render women especially prone.
Breuer and Freud, Studies on Hysteria, trans. by James Stratechy, 1895

I have bin told that after some hours I get my German language through speaking it very badly, [end is missing]
Anna O. / Bertha Pappenheim, from her own account of her illness, written in English (1882)

Lace is never for lace's sake. It is a way to tell a story.
Hildur Bjarnadóttir

Spitzen

for tatted lace   or *occhispitze*   you wind the thread

around a shuttle   which then   between fingers   back & forth

then up   &   down   so that   ring & arc-shaped   figures also

eye-loops   join   &   one below the other

into larger patterns   like a crest   in the blink of an eye

(gaze   into the candle)   (direkt in die flamme)

Doily with rings and chains for beginners (second round):
1. r. 3ds—p—3ds—p
1. ch. 6ds—p—3ds—p—3ds—p—6ds

bei der occhispitze   oder augenspitze   wickelt man den faden

auf ein schiffchen   welches zwischen   fingern   hin u her

welches auf u ab   so dass   ring u bogen förmige figuren auch

augen   schlaufen   verbunden   u untereinander zu

größeren formen   wie wellenkämme   augenblicke

(in die kerze schaun)   (strait into se flame)

Deckchen aus Ringen und Bogen für Anfänger (vierte Runde):
1. Rg. 12 a 12
1. Bg. 3 – 3 – 3 – 3 – 3 – 3 – 3 – 3

Tatting Shuttle.

the tatting shuttle   or   *schiffchen der augenspitze*

is thumb-sized   & resembles   a   small fold

mon dieu   *une petite occhi-pussy*   with which she can   or can't

(not really)   skip   but slip   *how d'you do* knots

as a lady of the upper   in day   or candle   light   and if she pulled

first   the   rascals   then the threads   from this folding   shuttle

do they   crochet or *yea*   unspool themselves

into certain shapes   entwined   or   deferred

such delicate &   slender textures   (auto-

Tatting Shuttle.

the tatting shuttle   oder   schiffchen der augenspitze

ist daumengroß   u ähnelt   einer   kleinen scheide

mon dieu   ein occhifötzchen   kann sie damit   damit kann sie

zwar nicht   hüpfen   aber   *knötgen   knüpffen*

als dame der oberen   bei tages   oder kerzen   licht   u zöge

nach   den   bälgern   fäden   aus dem scheiden schiffchen

spulen sich die   garne   oder   gerne   nach gewissen

mustern   verschlungene   oder   gestundete

zarte   u   schmale   gewebe   (auto-

suggestion)   it has also been   suggested etc.   unklar   the origin

of the wort tatting for making lace for wenn man einen faden placed

of cotton   oder leinen   by means of a   hand shuttle   pu tat ively

tatters mean   rags   with scandinavian roots   b u t (it has

also been suggested etc.)   while they sit   at their lace-work   chit

chatting the women tattled and gossiped but die origin ist nicht very

Grimm: *tattern, s. dattern*: the geese walk and chatter. *CREIDIUS* 1, 300

suggestion)   it has also been   suggested usw. unklar   der ursprung

des wortes tatting   for making lace by looping a thread   of cotton

or linen   by   means of a   hand   shuttle   man sagt tat   sächlich

steht tat ters   für fetzen mit skandinavischen wurzeln   b u t (it has

also been suggested usw.)   während sie   an ihren spitzen   sitzen

wie the women tattled   and gossiped aber die herkunft   is not very

Grimm: *tattern*, s. *dattern*: die gänse gehen und tattern miteinander. *CREIDIUS* 1, 300

1.—Pine Pattern Collar in Tatting.

w anna say   a pine pattern collar   ist der name

für lace   a moving face   made by me   or

by means of repeating   holes   (ear) pierce

&   close   those never   tired   mouths like

die   frauen tattern   die schiffchen   rattern   their teeth

what did they   tattle about   what did they   need etc.

1.—Pine Pattern Collar in Tatting.

in annan worten   pine pattern collar in tatting   is a name

for a lace   a moving face   made by me   or

means of repeating   holes   (ohr) öffnen

u   schließen   niemals   müder   münder wie

the women tattled the shuttles rattled their teeth

what did they tattle about   what did they   need etc.

(ear) ist gossip eine form von noise like tattern is stuttering   getting

stuck   the tongue behind teeth or hands within threads or thin *spinn*

fäden   or movable parts   is looping shuttles   eine form von

konversation   or   konversion

w anna say   a pine stutter collar   with   rolling *occhi*

is   or   us   converting   conversion disorder   into order

(ohr) is gossip a form of lärm   wie dattern   ist stottern stoßen

der zunge an zähne oder   hände an   fäden oder gossamer wings

or movable parts   ist schiffchen schlingen   eine form von

konversation   oder   konversion

in other words   pine stotter collar   mit   occhi

is or us   converting   conversion disorder   into order or tatting   with its double patter   of the tongue's   piercing tip

against the ridge   is a looping sound   for leaping round

how language tongue-ties itself in the alveolar tap or tapping into this

voice of   an other anna   when she was in her head   there was

"a sharp   and quiet observer   who observed   that foolish stuff"

oder tattern   mit dem doppel schlag   der zungen   spitze

an den gaumen ist ein schlaufenlaut   zum   lauschen   wie sich

sprache selber   ertappt   by the alveolar tap   or tapped into this

the sound made by   another anna   wenn sie in ihrem kopf war da

„ein scharfer und ruhiger beobachter der sich das   tolle   zeug ansah"

does she maybe want to say   **from the old german**   **word**

dattern or   tattern   two roads fork   1) to the chattering   geese

2) to the tattering   i.e. jittering   i.e. also quieter   doters

(&   how)   spinsterly   a tiny   tatting shuttle   cuts

its swathe through both   with threads   such slender nets

in twined textures &   it catches a little   catches a   a jitter

& it takes   it   it   to the schnattering geese   loops it it

round the tattering shes   one more knoten   says die zitternde

frau   then i did   my sorrows   into a hole

(& how) allay

will sie viel leicht sagen   von dem alten dt.   wort dattern oder tattern

führn zwei wege   1) zu den   schnatternden   gänsen   2) zu den

tatternden   d.h. zitternden   d.h. auch leiseren   greisen

(u   wie) gespinst   schlägt   zwischen beiden   ein kl.

tatting shuttle   seine schneisen mit   fäden   so schmalen ver

netzten geweben u fängt sich was   fängt   ein   ein zittern

bringt es es   den schnatternden gänsen   schlingt es es

um die   tatternden frauen   one more schlaufe   says the shaking

woman   dann habch   mein leiden   in ein loch

   (u   wie) gebannt

or   does   *freud*   want   to   say   (but   doesn't   say   )

if   you   speak   of   the   eye   of   a   needle

language   begins to   totter   lays eyes on you   like the sea

look here an eyelet   is œillet   is an öhr   for seeing

the eye of a sailor   the seemann ties the knot   & later dreams a lot

(when scrubbing the deck) of the beauty of loops in every harbour he

gives a lady his lace   for her (neck)   rough as rope &   coarse as cord

he sends the shuttle's work around   the world   (how very becoming)

in france as *frivolité*   in estonia it's called   *süstikpitsi*

(freud asks: how does such a camel fit through the needle's öhr?)

oder   will   *freud*   sagen   (sagt   er   nicht   )

spricht   man   von   nadel   öhren

kommt   sprache ins   schaukeln schaut einen   an   wie das meer

schaut her ein öhr   ist œillet   ist eyelet   it lets us see

the eye of a sailor   der seemann knüpft ösen   träumt später beim

(deck wischen) von der schönheit   der knoten   schenkt in jedem

hafen einer dame seine spitze   rau aus tau u   dick aus strick er

schickt die schiffchen arbeit   durch die   welt   (wo sie sich gehört)

in frankreich als *frivolité*   in estland   heißt sie   *süstikpitsi*

(freud fragt: wie kann ein solches kamel durch das nadelöhr?)

Tatting-Shuttle.

is called *süstikpitsi süstikpitsi* **syllables repeat** **like little shuttles**

through secret eyelets etc. in how many endless loops does she dream

of *departure* **in how many languages** **do the ropes of the sailor**

(as a matter of lace) coil **& is it called** *working on the little ship*

in departing translation **but t t in french** **(my little lip)**

like a slip of the tongue sl sl **sloped breakwater is it a** *frivolité*

in the sense of care free **(tho with so much care** **was made) or**

fragile **(because the end** *très fragile* **bends)** **or**

crumbled **because of latin** *friare* **like crumbling**

of the indo-germanic **tribe** **from ↘drilling** **belongs (to it)**

[with tools sharpened and laced, handle it, cut, then hit, kill, the board, bordure, bordello, bread crumbs]

Tatting-Shuttle.

heißt sie *süstikpitsi süstikpitsi* wiederhole die silben wie schiffchen

durch heimliche ösen usw. in wie vielen bögen träumt eine

vom *ablegen* in wie vielen sprachen winden sich (tat

sache) die seile des seemanns u heißt sie nach dem übersetzen

arbeit am schiffchen abrr eben auf französisch (mein kl. bisschen)

wie ein versprecher prrr prr wellenbrecher ist sie eine *frivolité*

im sinne von leicht fertig (wo das so bedacht gemacht) oder

zerbrechlich (weil das ende *très fragile* wände) oder

zerrieben weil doch lateinisch *friare* wie zerreiben

der indogermanischen sippe von ↘bohren (dahin) *gehört*

[mit scharfem oder spitzem werkzeug bearbeiten, pflügen, schlagen, töten, brett, bord,
bordell, brosame]

103 Spitzen Deutsch

or in some   languages or regional dialects "spitze"   also means

"pierce"   & "spit"   &   now no longer with sealed lips

the lace-stitching girls: form holes   between

white threads   or form silences   between   strains of saliva

or   an unformed silence   also disputed   i need to

puke   cecilia   i said   i have to   swallow it &

conversely   lace would mean "spitting"   silently in stitches

for (botched up) hours   having a pinch of hunger   would then mean

"to stuff

      lace"

oder heißt in manchen   ihrer mund- oder landarten   speichel

„spitze"   u speien „spitzen"   u   nu das mündige   an spitze

stickenden mädchen   sind zwischen weißen fäden   gebildete

löcher   oder zwischen   speichel fäden   gebildete

stille   oder ungebildete stille   auch gebrochen   ich muss mal

brechen cäcilie sagt ich   muss es runter   schlucken anders

rum heißt   spitzen „speien"   in schweigend verstickten

(vergeigten) stunden   einen hunger leiden   aber heißt

„spitze

     schlingen"

so that the loopholes   in their high relief

carry   two or four main   threads   that eventually

(what is relief) diminish   so that at arrival   as opposed to

departure   (no avail) very subtle contours   (a veil) so that

after all the looping   the faden is to be pulled tight very gently

or after all the chaining   the father has to play right with the gentry

because   they are his picots   yes are his   *brides à picot*

attractive ties   for old age &   for diminishing its weight

so dass sie beim über schlingen   der hohen reliefs

zwei vier leit fäden   mitführen   die sich allmählich

(what is relief) verringern   so dass beim anlangen   im gegensatz

zum ablegen   ganz feine umrisse   (schleier) so dass

nach der schlingenbildung   der faden mit der nadel anzuziehen oder

nach der ringbildung   der vater mit dem adel anzuzieren   denn

sie sind   die bogenpicots   ja sie sind die   *brides à picot*

reizvolle verknüpfungen für alte tage u deren schwere dann zu mildern

& that's how it's put   t'gether   one   entry reads

"i wanted to lace into him"   but owing   to her double vision

it was decided to lace her up instead   with   her piercing eye

lace   she peeks between fingers   back & forth   what

up & down   wasn't the shuttle   a second mouth   & the

white animal full of holes   on the shirt   a handle   that she flies off

that she conducts herself every hour   always along the threading trace

yes   so long   this body   a lie   a   gap she carries with her

u so wird das zsmn   gesetzt   ein   eintrag ist

„ich wolt dir wohl die spitzen weisen"   aber da   sie doppelt sah

wollt man   sie lieber ein   weisen   mit   ihrer augen

spitze   schaut sie   zwischen fingern   hin u her   welch

auf und ab   war nicht das schiffchen   ein zweiter mund u das

lückenhafte weiße tier   auf dem hemd   ein häutchen das sie aus

u auf   führt   jede volle stunde   immer am tracierfaden   lang

ja so lang   dieser körper   eine lüge   eine lücke   die mit ihr geht

IV.

Cold
Kitchen

BOUGAINVILLEA

I

mis-dotted morning, how it rises in the mist,
how the blotting paper soaks, watercolors,
incline of leaf tips, or inclined towards tipped-in tulle,
a branchling peels out of its costume, has no
body, uncurls itself, takes its pick (green) and
the nerve endings in the shoulder of the valley
welcome this, they move their arms, wave to the
table, the knots, blossoms, the ungraspable air—

BOUGAINVILLE

I

vertüpfelter morgen, wie er unterm nebel aufsteigt,
wies unterm löschblatt durchweicht, wasserfarben
hang aus blattspitzen und hang zu zipfelndem tüll,
schält sich ein ästlein aus dem kostüm, hat keinen
körper, streckt sich, besinnt sich auf (grün) und die
nervenenden in der schulter des tals begrüßen das,
bewegen ihren arm, sie heben die hand zum tisch,
zu den knoten, blüten, der nicht zu fassenden luft –

II

lacking stipules, lacking graspable foundations
around you; and is therefore this lignified scheme
a crime scene of description, membranous, ribbed,
the style often spangled with papillae, do you get it,
without looking, tangled only in the collision of vowels
between hairs, thorns, how this is overgrown, can you bring
it home, the carpel's seam split into lanceolate leaves, can
you copy that, in the signals' hybrid twittering—

II

fehlen nebenblätter, fehlen fassliche gründe um
dich herum und ist dieses verholzene komplott
ein tatort der beschreibung, häutig, rippig, sind
so oft die griffel besetzt mit papillen, kapier das,
ohne ein anschauen, ausgesetzt allein dem anprall
der vokale zwischen haaren, stacheln, lässt es sich
verwachsen, lässt sich einheimsen, zipfliger saum
samt etwa lanzettlicher spreite, kopier das, im
                    zwittern der signale –

III

found ovate bracts, found islands by the wayside today,
cut both ways, luminously triangular, how closely could
you circumnavigate them, whose hands disguised as sailors
could grasp them, pinnate veins and well-stuffed akene,
possibly pressed, weren't you stranded in the planted air,
with your collector's mouth and colors unloaded as goods,
as guides, how this hedges, and in a word: en-shrubs you—

III

finde eiförmige hochblätter, finde heute am wegrand
noch inseln, zweideutig, vieläugig leuchtend, aus
welcher nähe wären sie umsegelt, mit welchen händen,
als seemann gekleidet, wären sie verstanden, paarige
beutel und pralle stände, wie gepresst, warst du nicht
gestrandet in der ausgesetzten luft, sammelnder mund
und umschlag von farbe in ware, in wahnsinn, wie das
weiterheckt und dich mit einem wort: einsträuchert –

IV

once the eyes are out on stalks, tell me how the filaments travel,
scrambling over bricks, fences, lips, nets of small explosives, or
plosives, try it, right here, dot yourself, lips lobed and brittle skin,
fanning inward, loosely folding *paper-flowers*: source the name
to the island, say *solos* is a language where flower is *plaua*,
where one knows collisions, also such borrowings, the freight of
picked corollas—

IV

sag nach erstem augenübergehn wie fäden wandern,
sich verbreiten über mauern, zäune, lippen, netz aus
kleinen explosionen, oder plosiven, probier das, hier,
zier dich, mundstülpen und brüchige haut, oder nach
innen fächern, lose falten, *paperflowern*: folge dem
namen zur insel zurück, sag *solos* ist eine sprache,
die blume *plaua* nennt, aufprall kennt, auch solches
borgen, fracht gepflückter blüten –

one also hears the phrase "in die fichten gehen:" to get
into conifer straits, to be pulled up by the roots, to become
destitute
Grimm's dictionary

I
"scenic scenery." so, anyway: to pass around the burden,
branches weighed down with blankets of snow, little moan.
so the spruces don't break into silence. because Regen is
county seat, declines charge, le vivre et le couvert de neige.
accordingly: "the location is not our fault." only the confines
and brightness. the forest writes: "willkommen." the words
for this are white or gone like the last bus from the village.
at night stillness lumbers in chills: the forest for the foreign

The allocation . . . ought to facilitate the readiness to return to the
homeland.
Art. 6, para. 5 of the Bavarian Asylum Implementation Ordinance

DREI BÖGEN : BÖBRACH

man hört auch: in *die fichten gehen,* **verloren gehen,**
wegkommen
Grimmsches Wörterbuch

I

„ländlicher landstrich". also lasten verteilen, schneedecken
schichten auf ästen, kleines ächzen. dass auch die fichten
nicht brechen ins schweigen. denn regen ist kreisstadt, nei-
gen pflicht. entsprechend: „für die lage können wir nichts."
nur für die grenzen und den hellen schein. der forst ist rein,
„it welcomes you". die worte dazu sind weiß oder weg wie der
letzte bus aus dem dorf. nachts rumpelt die stille im frost: der
wald sei dem fremden

Die Verteilung ... soll die Bereitschaft zur Rückkehr in das Heimatland
fördern
DVAsyl Bayern § 6 Abs. 5

II

"not unreasonable." like wallpaper, where only the eyes wander. like you can't see the would for the trees, they hand out no papers to you. but promise permits entry soon, and then there's stammering at the way station. night, the giant cell, bars and unbars itself. inside the hammering, in here the crease: "schauen bauen schneien freuen." this language once was firn, then holidaythingamajig, it sure beams everybody back home. and where's that supposed to be: "don't care a tittle," but the schnapps, the schnapps, just a little

II

„zumutbar". wie wallpaper, wo nur die augen wandern. wie
einer am andern die stämme, sie stammen von hier, reichen
dir keine papiere. aber einreißen bald, und steht ein stam-
meln an der haltestelle. oder nacht, die große zelle, sperrt
sich selber auf und zu. drin das hämmern, drin die stirn:
„schauen bauen schneien freuen." diese sprache war mal
firn, dann feriendings, die leuchtet jeden heim. und wo soll
das sein: „schnurz". aber bärwurz, bärwurz,

III

paints the scene in the sense of whitewash, or a lustrous
façade burns in your eyes. who knows a joke about ever-
green fences, who will see the greener side when "in dis-
tress they shed their needles." so, cut the cord, the snow
is bored, the old keep: "exclusively branded goods." cold
supplies, one another into the mouth, as long as they last.
beyond the snow blankets still zero reception. only the for-
est bureau forages duties, is up to no good, he takes you in
white quoted frogmarch.

III

ein rändlicher anstrich im sinne von land, oder glänzender
wandsinn brennt dir im kopf. wer kennt ein gespräch über
fichten, wen fichts an, wenn „bei stress fallen die nadeln eher
ab". also abnabeln, schnee adeln, die alte unterkunft: „alles
markenware". kalte päckchen, einander in den mund, so-
lange sie reichen. überm deckchen derweil null empfang.
nur der wald treibt sein stöberndes amt, er nimmt dich in
weiße abführungszeichen.

COLD KITCHEN

My language and I, we don't talk to each other, we have nothing to say to each other. I know what I have to know—it likes cold food better than warm food, not even the coffee is supposed to be hot. This can really keep you busy.
Ilse Aichinger, My Language and I

Cold soup, cold soup clear and particular and a principal a principal question to put into.
Gertrude Stein, Tender Buttons

I

so goes the fairy tale, which they served us, steaming, a dish: those were the days when The Wishing-Table was still around to help. a sort of direct connection with the thing, set thyself, the right phrase hauled out all its stock, hearty, the land famous for its magic nosh. the gap between food, thought, mouth, and hand was slight enough that no one fell into it or mistook themselves for another, who fed them. the dishes never piled up—after all, there was only a dash of the same thing for everyone.

KALTE KÜCHE

Was ich wissen muß, weiß ich, kalte Küche ist ihr lieber
als warme, nicht einmal der Kaffee soll heiß sein. Das be-
schäftigt einen schon.
Ilse Aichinger, Meine Sprache und ich

Cold soup, cold soup clear and particular and a principal a
principal question to put into.
Gertrude Stein, Tender Buttons

I

ging das märchen, das man uns vorsetzte, dampfend, ein
gericht: waren tage, als das tischlein noch geholfen hat. eine
art direktverbindung mit dem ding, deck dich, das rechte
wort fuhr schüsseln auf, deftig, land bekanntlich im zau-
bermampf. so gering der abstand zwischen speis, gedanke,
mund und hand, dass niemand hineinfiel oder sich für eine
andere hielt, die sie fütterte. nie türmte abwasch, allerdings –
es gab nur einwas für alle.

II

but the days came when the stock phrases multiplied. gaps
grew bigger, some fell into them, got stuck in each oth-
er's head, with foreignness. even so, the stock remained
depleted, *little table*, nicht more. instead, menus with ambig-
uous watermarks began to hover over everything—faded
lists, sloshing softly. each was an enchanted inventory, each
measured the perceived distance, resistance from the thing.
or so they said. where concord was held, where songs were
once yelled, there now glimmered jelly-like things. jelly-like
things. sometimes it helped to repeat things thrice, like in
equally wobbly times.

II

kamen aber tage, als die schüsselworte sich vermehrten.
abstände wuchsen, man fiel hinein, man hatte einander und
fremdes im ohr. die schüsseln blieben leer, tischlein: no more.
stattdessen schwebten über allem speisekarten mit unein-
deutigen wasserzeichen, blasse listen, die sanft schwappten.
jede, hieß es, war verwunschenes inventar, jede maß die kühl
empfundene entfernung, entkernung vom ding. wo einklang
gegolten, wo lieder gegellt hatten, schimmerte gallertartiges.
gallertartiges. manchmal half es, wie in ähnlich sämigen
zeiten, worte dreimal zu sagen.

III

nevertheless, no one wandered in want. they only longed
for the good old boiled and grainy things, framed by ears of
golden wheat, also sweet mush, stirred by a homely hand.
because all digesting, discerning was trained on this kind
of feast: speech, thought—one lump. they wanted to fatten
in quiet now, to scrounge later. they said even the chief bard
with his red pennant asked for the sash to be re-labelled,
called himself barbel, became fish of the year, a catch. but
none of the trawling whippersnappers got to the bottom of
his muteness.

III

man wanderte darum nicht darbend. man sehnte nur
gesottnes und korn zurück, ährenkränze, auch süßen brei,
von heimischer hand gerührt. denn alles verdauen, verste-
hen sei an dieser art schmaus geschult: rede, gedanke – ein
topf. man wolle also in stille mästen, sich später durch-
fressen. sogar der hauptbarde mit seinem roten wimpel, hieß
es, ließ die schärpe umbeschriften, nannte sich barbe, ward
fisch des jahres, wurde fang. doch keiner von den jungen
fischersspunden kam je seiner stummheit auf den grund.

IV

so the fairy tale goes, nearly self-frothingly ever after, chew-
ing, ahead of us. but the truth is we were well-versed in other
arts: cold kitchen. we knew of parents in secret brigades
who never gave in to a table they hadn't equipped them-
selves—and be it not a table, and only a tablecloth, or not
even that. near the coast the picnic brigades, turned toward
the surf; the folding-brigades with their alms of fans, mul-
tipli, lastly a state-of-the-garnish brigade. they all stole the
garde manger's knowledge via detours, smuggling, re-dis-
tributing. their plates were color palettes, permuted, mari-
nated: vol-au-vent, worlds on distraction. oh basil, plucked
razzle-dazzle, oh sails of their sandwich frigates: they
steered towards us.

IV

ging das märchen, nahezu selbstschäumend, kauend, uns
vor. dabei kannten wir andere künste, kalte küchen. wir
wussten von eltern in geheimen brigaden, die nie einem tisch
erlagen, den sie nicht eigenhändig bestückt, und sei es kein
tisch, nur tuch, und sei es nicht einmal tuch. an küsten die
picknickbrigaden, brandungsgewandt, die faltbrigaden mit
ihren fächergaben, multipli, schließlich brigade garnier cri.
sie stahlen den gardemanger wissen über umwege, schmug-
gelten ein, verteilten. ihre platten waren farbpaletten, per-
mutiert, mariniert: vol-au-vent, welten auf ablenkung. oh
basilikum, gezupftes dideldum, die segel ihrer schnittenfre-
gatten sie steuerten uns an.

V

news from the unheated, unfounded regions, which we received. how do you fill the space left behind by a pit, a green orbit, a nest of capers? the answer is salty, like snow-sprinkled clams: why don't you make a mess and dress it until no one fancies an entrée anymore. they take us for garnishers, but really we're diminishers, our food guest-pectant, a *gap gardening*—every neighborly french-fried radish amuses, flourishingly, a displaced mouth. in the gaps, there are things still fusioniering today, if they're not salvaged before—for other fables, otherwise hungry foibles.

V

nachrichten aus ungewärmten gegenden, unbegründeten, die wir erhielten. wie füllt man den raum, den ein kern hinterlässt, grüne ferne, ein kapernnest? die antwort salzig, auf muscheln getupfter schnee: richtet sachen an, bis niemand mehr hauptgang verlangt. man hält uns für verzierer, doch sind wir deplacierer, unsere kost gastwartend, ein gap garden – jede in nachbarliche friese geschnitzte radiese amüsiert, blühend, einen verschobenen mund. in abständen mingeln, wenn nicht geborgen, noch heute für andere märchen, sonst hungrige närrchen.

V.

Babeltrack (Notes on a Lengevitch)

In fact, wir sein ready,
Was das anconzernt.
Kurt M. Stein, <u>Die schönste Lengevitch</u>, 1925

137

february 16. white balloon, white and milky with days built in honeycombs, stillness in everything, breast-days and carrying-days, a child in my head without language, no, a child in my head with a language, but unwritten, no delivery for this lingua-child, honeycombed days, carrying days, complected white and white with mice teeth at the fringes, such crochet things, slings, loops and bubbles built in saliva, be-sputtered, a-babbled, meaning a sort of air-bubble-speak, cheering and clicking, balloon-like, without skeins, for which no notation, connotation, for which no makeshift lodging, no arrival unless evening, a vale evening, a landing alight on extended ribbit, in valley-ripples of frog-throats, hovering above is this stitched closeness, milk-cheeked and indistinguishable because without speech, says someone who doesn't need to know ...

16. februar. weißer ballon, weißer milchiger mit wabenarti-
gen tagen, stille in allem, brust- und tragetage, ein kind im
kopf, das keine sprache, falsch, ein kind im kopf, das sprache
hat, die nicht geschrieben, keine niederkunft für dieses
sprachenkind, wabenartige tage, tragetage, verwebtes weiß
und weiß mit mäusezähnen am rand, gehäkeltes material,
schlingen und blasen im speichel gebildet, gebubbelt, geb-
abelt, also z.b. luftblasensprache, jauchzen und schnalzen,
ballonartig, ohne stränge, für das keine notation, konnota-
tion, für das keine notunterkunft, keine ankunft, es sei denn
abende, talabende, ein landen im langhin gequakten, in tal-
wogen aus froschkehlen, und darüber diese nähe, milchwan-
gig, verwechselbar, weil ohne sprache, sagt einer, der es nicht
wissen muss ...

being on an island, having a child, writing, and having a child as the reverse of insularity, namely: becoming archipelago, the edges swell up, are made permeable, build new mainlands for nourishment—ferries en route until the morning, leaving milk-trails behind, milk-trails and fringed sleep-veils so that the mainlands snooze again, loosened from everything; and the language of this island makes calor, and the language of the child still makes sucking-sounds, soon speech-sounds, and in the snippet-language of the one typing among them bubbles form and things get picked up, and in one bubble swims jakobson, saying: children with their wild sounds, with their first blustering babble, are able to produce any imaginable sound of any language, the bubble rises, which they'll soon forget, the bubble floats pregnant with meaning above the afternoon, once they acquire their mother tongue, the bubble pops

auf einer insel sitzen, ein kind haben, schreiben, kindhaben
das gegenteil von verinselung, nämlich archipel werden, die
ränder schwemmen auf, werden durchlässig, bilden neue
festländer für versorgungen – fähren unterwegs bis in den
morgen, ziehen milchbahnen hinter sich her, milchbahnen
und fransige schlafbänder, so dass auch die festländer wie-
der dösen, sich lösen von allem, und in der sprache der insel
macht es warm, in der sprache des kindes macht es noch
sauglaut, bald sprachlaut, in der schnipselsprache der mit-
tendrin tippenden schlagen blasen, werden sachen aufge-
lesen, steht in einer blase jakobson, sagt: die kinder mit ihren
wilden lauten, mit dem ersten blusteren lallen, sind sie in der
lage, alle denklichen laute aller sprachen zu erzeugen, blase
steigt auf, welche sie dann vergessen, blase schwebt bedeu-
tungsschwanger überm mittag, wenn sie ihre muttersprache
lernen, platzt

there are grounds grounding the trail of game passes, or deer crossings, or cheers crossing into other sounds, or the criteria for the *chose* of ethnic identity or contentment, or doubts about ethnic belonging or contentment would be like pains in teething, phantom-like wreathing, not yet formed, invisible pulling and wrenching in the gums, a ripple in the roof opening to mouth-sky, where something both constructs and dismantles itself, such un-shingling, i lack it this ring-thing, kling-e-ling, which when it changes is wild and not yet trail, it fails me this not-yet-known-but-almost-one, the known-and-lost-again-one, the humming quickly gone, the empty-dent-of-sort, the other-words-inviting-snort, and all these words then pounce on each other, the different kind, wild and not child, they're in cahoots inside my head, these failing trails, exultant foreign arrangement of folds, folds are falten, me falta, es fehlt mir, this word, which means miss, in the language of this island, in another *fala* is "i speak"— a spark, a faltering unresting sway; en-wringed

dem wildwechsel oder lautwechsel liegen gründe zu grunde,
die kriterien zur wald der ethnischen identität oder zufrie-
denheit oder zweifel an der ethnischen zugehörigkeit oder
zufriedenheit wären schmerzen beim zahnen, phantom-
artiges bahnen, nicht ausgebildetes, nicht sichtbares zie-
hen und zerren im gaumen, riffel im munddach, öffnung auf
mundhimmel zu, aufbau und gleichzeitiger abbau von was, es
fehlt mir, das ringding, tingeling, welches, das wechselt, wild
und nicht in der spur, fehlt mir das noch nicht gewusste, aber
schon wahrgenommene wort, auch das gewusste und wie-
der vergessene fort, das summende womm, das leere hinter-
lassende snort, das darum andere worte einladende of sort,
wo sie dann übereinander herfallen, die andere sorte, wild
und nicht kind, fremde frohlockende faltenwürfe, *falta* heißt
fehlen in der sprache dieser insel, *fala* sprich in einer andern,
machen im kopf gemeinsame sache, fehlentwürfe, ein ent-
fachen, unruhe falterndes schwanken, verwringen sich

february 17. wanted to come steal the child from the cra-
dle, i lay restless, fidgety hem tip and tail, beside her, fright-
sleeper, blinked awake into the half-lit (one blind open, the
same frog-chant wave-like from the valley, just past midnight
and the lantern at the garden gate a white lightish moth, the
lights across the valley more yellowish, then velvety, eye-ex-
pansive dark), and i listened, poised, predicting knistern,
rustle, hush-hush stealthy steps in the adjoining room, the
adherent outside, the adjacent night, but why steal a child,
why take my child, my eye-clarity and little nit, why in this
dell, well, people came like this, heavy like this, and their
coming was bells and hawk-hooding, looming clouds and
clusters of fears around my head, so scared again that they
would come and steal all sounds, so that i nestled up against
the latticed cot, next to my bed, and looked at the child,
eye-fastened, ear-pricked, and her almost inaudible body
breath, was like this, light like this, and then i squeezed my
arm through the little bars, hand on chest, a dab

17. februar. wollte man kommen, das kind aus der wiege steh-
len, ich lag unruhig, zipfelig daneben, schreckschlaf, wach-
geblinzelt ins zimmerhalbdunkel (ein fensterladen offen,
froschsang wellenartig aus dem tal, bis kurz nach zwölf die
laterne vorm garten weißlichtig und falterhaft, gelblicher
die lampen auf der anderen talseite, dann samtiges, augen-
weitendes dunkel), und ich lauschte, mir wahnte knistern,
heimliche schritte im nebenzimmer, im nebendraußen, im
nachtneben, aber warum wollte man ein kind stehlen, mein
kind nehmen, mein augenklar und federling, warum in die-
sem tal, egal, das kommen der leute war so, schwer so, läutete
und häubte wie wolkendräue oder angsttrauben um meinen
kopf, schreckte mich so wieder, dass sie kommen, alle laute
stehlen, bis ich mich schmiegte ans littlegitter, das neben
meinem bett, und das kind anschaute, blickheft, ohrgespitzt,
ihr kleiner, fast unhörbarer körperatem, war so, leicht so,
und zwängte endlich meinen arm durch gitterstäbe, ihr die
hand auf die brust, getupft

*the dissolution of the linguistic sound system in aphasics provides
an exact mirror-image for the phonological development in child
language*, **writes jakobson, writes** *for* **and not** *of,* **as if aphasia
made the child's acquisition of speech possible in the first
place and with it every production of sound in developmen-
tal stages, as if it held the mirror or provided rules, folie oder
folly, as if we could find in this very bad sound-production
disorder a blueprint for what is to come, or this blueprint
would be a berry print, at least in spain, where the pronun-
ciation rules demand that very bad is berry bad, where the
disordered blueprint becomes blur-print, where the picks,
smudges or shifts of red and blue spheres dictate a pattern
into the hedge, where they cloud thicket, light-locks, iris-
gaps, irritant traps, through which all me slips in, even light-
work, plait and crochet lights, blankets that the child sees,
at which the child stares as if by mesmer surprised,**

der abbau des sprachlichen lautbestandes bei den aphasischen liefert
das genaue spiegelbild für den lautlichen aufbau der kindersprache,
schreibt jakobson, schreibt interessanterweise nicht: apha-
sischer abbau liefert spiegelbild *des* kindlichen aufbaus,
schreibt: *für,* als ob die aphasische störung das kindliche
und damit jedes sich in entwicklung befindliche lautbauen
erst möglich machte, spiegel hielte oder spielregel lieferte,
folie oder folly, als ob wir in der very bad lautbaustörung
die blaupause fänden für noch kommendes, oder eine
blaupause wäre eine beerenpause, jedenfalls in spanien, wo
die aussspracheregeln verlangen, dass very bad sich berry
bad spricht, wo die gestörte blaupause zur beerenpause
wird, wo die gepflückten oder verrückten roten oder blauen
kugeln ein muster in die hecke diktieren, wo sie dickichten,
blicklichten, irisierende oder irritierende lücken, durch die
alles meinliche einfällt, auch lichtwerk, flecht- und häkel-
lichter, decken, die das kind sieht, auf die das kind starrt wie
vom mesmer getroffen,

and instead one calls people without aphasia, but with a rather multilingual fantasia, with nothing broke in the broca and everything clicking in the wernicke, and who still—come the moment—wade through their mother tongue, plagued by such hard-word-finding, if they're not already swamped by the word hard-word-finding, now does one call this marginal competeasing or polymorph-stumbling in german *sprachabbau* or *-korrosion*, which means as much as and a bit like attrition, and first transfires in little access problems in conversations, i mean timing, a kind of conversation-smudging, where you must prepare for the blurprint, so as to get a blur or berry in, right, but you're just sitting there and others hevva juicy red chin

dagegen spricht man bei menschen, die nicht aphasieren, die eher mehrsprachig phantasieren, denen nichts bröckelt am broca, nichts wegnickt am wernicke, und die sich dennoch, kommt der tag, abbrechen einen in ihrer muttersprach, von wortfindungsschwierigkeiten geplagt, falls sie nicht schon verloren haben sich im wort wortfindungsschwierigkeiten, und nennt man dieses grenzkompetenzlern oder poly-morphholpern im englischen *attrition*, was so viel heißt und ein wenig wie abreibung, sich äußerlicht zuerst in kleinen zugangsproblemen bei gesprächen, ich meine timing, eine art gesprächspflücking, wo man die beerenpause schon vorahnen muss, hinsichtlich abzukriegen eine beere, nicht wahr, aber du sitzt nur so da und andere hef se saftig rote kinn

february 18. am i by the sea, let's say atlantic, and the child asleep warm slumbery in the shade, in the circular after-noon of a bast parasol with a rusty pole, asleep in the stroller bassinet, black, a black bassinet on bast mats, blonde, lying on black sand, held by round-smoothed stones, and the sand was carried here by the sea, was brought forth, or delivered, as pebbles or grains; anyway, thus-carried sand-kids, how everything's interlaced, in carrying-phrases and speech-bubbles, or am i now stuck in one, did i lose my way, let myself be led a-vey, ah weh where war ich, ach water, shall i go in, my first time in the atlantic, which lies so duti-fully uncurled, which so dutifully or dottifully nestles to the earth, shall i go in or not go in, do i stretch out my toes, is it cold, and do i want to say something, and do i say it, then i hear it: the water is too small,

18. februar. bin ich am meer, sagen wir atlantik, schläft das kind warm schlummerig im schatten, im kreisrunden nachmittag eines bastschirms, mit rostigem ständer, schläft in der ausgebauten tragetasche des kinderwagens, die schwarz, schwarze tasche auf bastmatten, blond, die auf schwarzem sand liegen, von rundgeschliffenen steinen gehalten, und den sand hat hergetragen das meer vor sich, hat ihn niedergelegt, oder lassen niederkommen, als kiesel oder körner, jedenfalls so getragene sandkiddies, alles ineinander verschackteltt, in tragephasen und sprachblasen, oder steck ich jetzt in einer fest, bin ich abgekommen, hab mich ahweh bringen lassen, ah weh wo wa ich, wasser, geh ich hinein, zum ersten mal in den atlantik, der artig glattgestrichen liegt, der sortig oder artig an die erde schmiegt, geh ich hinein oder geh ich nicht, streck die zehen vor, ist es kalt, will ich was sagen, sag ich es, höre: the water is too small,

and do these words come strangely out of my mouth, are cold in the manner of meaning but small in deed, and have a core of clang, the sound chain spills over into the meaning chain, because this sentence has an A where the german would have an A, but not the original english, not really, at least not if you wanted to say *kalt*, if you meant cold, och bloody old cold, guter alter ozean, which nabs me now, which grabscht my toes, propping up the language wave, and there a little bonnet dances, out of sheer As a little sonnet prances, then that's the long and shore of it, along which clatters over pebbles, a sheer of klackering baloney

kommen diese worte wunderlich aus meinem mund, sind im
meinen kalt, in der tat dagegen klein, und haben einen kern
aus klang, lautkette, schwappt über sinnkette, weil steht in
diesem englisch satz ein A, wo im deutschen steht ein A, im
englisch aber keins, jedenfalls nicht, wenn man will sagen cold,
wenn man meint cold, och olles cold, good old cold ouschn,
der mich erwischt, der meine zehe robbt, sprachwellen auf-
bockt, und tanzt darauf ein häubchen, aus lauter A's ein
stäubchen tanzt, ist das die gischt von es, am ufer klackert
über steine, lauter klackert kokolores

february 19. and could the en-wringing or finding-irritant of *cold* have its reasons, could have its tide switch after the code-switch, to be washed out or overfed, a processing center; dear madam, your possessing center lacks good guidance, or what about the concept of linguistic overgeneralization, where you adopt a learnt pattern in order to lop crooked morpho-matter, for instance: *go—i went, be—i bent*, so does this also apply to the lexis, is that why my form-ship sanked, and why a whole school of As was catched in the net, an A-generalization: *kalt* is small, *alt* is all, and for aphasics the sequence of attrition progresses like this: first the lexis, then the peripheral grammar, lastly, the core grammar, which was the first to be a-choired

19. februar. und könnte die verwringung oder irritierend
findung von kalt haben gründe, haben gezeitenwechsel nach
sprachwechsel, unterspült oder überfüttert sein ein rechenz-
entrum, liebe frau, ihrem hechelzentrum fehlt gute führung,
oder gibt es das konzept der übergeneralisierung beim verar-
beiten von sprachen, wo man ein gelerntes muster überträgt
und schiefe morphoformen sägt, zum beispiel gehen: ich
ging, sehen: ich sing, und gibt es das auch bei der lexik, ist
darum mir das formenschiff gesankt, ein ganzer schwall aus
A im netz gefangt, eine A-generalisierung: kalt ist small, alt
ist all, und bei aphasikern die reihenfolge des sprachverlusts
verhält sich so: zuerst die lexik, dann die periphere gram-
matik, schließlich die kerngrammatik, die man zuerst erwarf

but if i'm mistaken and my swimming brain brims not with overgeneralization but with overdetermination so that my small-and-not-cold-at-all ocean drifts to freud and his con-cept of overdetermined psychopathological symptoms, whose structures i borrow to write, to decide: where lan-guages (themes) stratify close to the nucleus and lead out-ward concentrically to produce the word (symptom), this smelting of languages (themes) develops distinctly bound-ary-crossing or foaming (irrational) attachments, by which i mean (freudlos now) a babble phase, in which words of all languages are imaginable, a smelt-speak or schmelzing of, a lengevitch, then that's the shore of it

wenn ich mich aber irre und mein schwimmend hirn
schwappt mir statt übergeneralisierung von überdetermin-
ierung was vor, so dass mein kleines statt kaltes meer zu freud
treibt und seinem konzept der überdeterminiertheit von
psychopathologischen symptomen, deren struktur ich mir
borge, um zu schreiben, zu entscheiden: wo sprachen (the-
men) in kernnähe sich miteinander vereinen und gemeinsam
nach außen führen, um dort das wort (symptom) zu erzeugen,
da entstehen bei der verschmelzung beider sprachen (the-
men) deutlich entgrenzende oder aufschäumende (irratio-
nale) anhaftungen, will sagen (freudless jetzt) eine lallphase,
in der worte aller sprachen vorstellbar sind, schmelzsprech
oder auslassing, eine lengevitch, ist sie die gischt von es

february 20. a break in the broadcast for an announcement, a breach in the surface of language, bouncing: fingertip alert! carefully felt in the child's mouth: first surfacing of bite, of grind, a tiny piercing of the gums in the lower jaw, after endless days of air-chopping, after chomping on what is yet to come, not quite visible, but visible enough for internal parental break-through-cooing, tooth-ache as secret time-ache, also an ach-ache, as the what's-to-come pushes about, flesh stretches without bleeding (is that why they're called *gummi*), drives out little white tooth-blossoms and then nestles again, for six years it nestles, blossom beside blossom in the jaw garden or little sound pasture with its four quadrants—two gentle sharp ones up front, and at the back the large-leaved ones like bright clover, milk molar cleaver, in between the spiky pines of canines, a garden for the tongue to meander, miniscule key-flowers for language, *laut*, unlocked

20. februar. unterbrechung der sendung für eine nachricht, durchbrechung der unmittelbaren sprachschicht: fingerspitzenalarm! gefühlt mit kuppe im kindermund: erste schneidefläche, reibefläche, winziges durchstoßen des zahnfleischs im unterkiefer, nach tagelangem indielufthauen, herumkauen auf kommendem, sichtbar noch nicht, sichtbar genug für inneres elterliches durchbruchsgurren, zahnweh als heimliches zeitweh, auch ahweh, wie kommendes schiebt herum, fleisch sich blutlos teilt (als ob es darum heißt: gums), austreibt weiße zahnblütchen und anschmiegt sich wieder, sechs jahre lang anschmiegt, blüte um blüte im kiefergarten oder lautackerchen mit seinen vier quadranten, vorne zwei zarte scharfe, hinten die großblättrigen, heller milchmolarklee, dazwischen spitze hecken der eckzähne, ein garten für die zunge zum spazieren, winzige schlüsselblumen zur sprache, laute, unlocked

february 21. molars, myriad mobiles—star, and the child sleeps in her bed again, and around it a valley, volley or voll it may be called, where i practice my blicken through palm-gaps, berry bad and anderersights, while the frog-track ripples through the banana valley, quack-quack, with its multi-tracked croaking surrounding the child, who grows, and i now at her bed, encircling attrition, the spot where structures collapse and where the surface cracks, some-thing for becoming permeable, for a napping tooth to nag, with quadrants, querulants, for the babeltrack in the trail-vale, ribbit, repeat, repeat

21. februar. molare, unzählige mobilés – stern, und schläft das kind im bett again, und liegt ein tal darum, das wallt oder walleh heißt, wo ich mein blicking durch palmenlücken treib, berrybad und otherweiß, derweil der froschtrack im bananental ribbelt, ribbit, sein mehrspuriges quaken noch das kind umgibt, das wächst, und ich an seinem bett, das abreiben umkreisend, die abreibestelle, die doch eine aufreibestelle, für was zum durchlassen, zum zahn im schlaf wachsen, mit quadranten, querulanten, für babeltrack im bahnental, repeat, repeat

VI.

Drives Across a Bridge, Is a Bridge, Hums:

Texts on Translation

Messages from a Beehive: On Translating from Belarusian

But the mother of vowels slumps from my throat
like the queen of a havocked beehive.
Valzhyna Mort

My relationship with Belarusian buzzes like a beehive. My relationship with Belarusian has flown off. My relationship with Belarusian bears the names of poets I translated: Volha Hapeeva, Maryja Martysewitsch, Vera Burlak, Vika Trenas, Valzhyna Mort. My relationship with Belarusian hums like a train. My relationship with Belarusian is that I don't speak Belarusian. My relationship with Belarusian bears the names of translators I've worked with: Katharina Narbutovic, Irina Gerassimowitsch, Martina Mrochen, André Böhm. My relationship with Belarusian is double-tracked and never direct. My relationship with Belarusian is a flight of fancy.

My relationship with Belarusian is a sleeping car with a broken samovar. Crane light in the night, echoes on the factory floor. At the border my relationship with Belarusian is lifted up and receives a new bogie. Perhaps my relationship with Belarusian will always veer. My relationship with Belarusian is indisposed to sporting. My relationship with Belarusian leapfrogs over other kinds of backs. In third grade my relationship with Belarusian receives Russian lessons. At 25 my relationship with Belarusian learns Polish. Once in Minsk my relationship with Belarusian is a diplomat who swallows three spoonfuls of vegetable oil before every meeting and says, every third toast is to Love.

My relationship with Belarusian hums drunkenly. My relationship with Belarusian veers home into its room at the October Hotel in Minsk. My relationship with Belarusian is a nightly view from the thirteenth floor. Floodlight on empty streets, cold sun city, hard shadows in the government quarter. At the attempt to photograph my relationship with Belarusian from the thirteenth floor, the lens hits the glass and never shuts again. My relationship with Belarusian underestimated the distance. My relationship with Belarusian must have forgotten to refuel diplomatic oil for vodka resistance. Since then my relationship with Belarusian has had a brown, a black, and a lame eye. Since then my relationship with Belarusian has had a tic in the upper eyelid. My relationship with Belarusian twitches. My relationship with Belarusian is going at full steam. At night my relationship with Belarusian stops between stations.

In the morning my relationship with Belarusian negotiates with the hotel's breakfast matron for a second cup of tea. That morning my relationship with Belarusian does not get its second cup of tea. Later my relationship with Belarusian becomes a futurist walk against the soaking gray high-rises. My relationship with Belarusian is a conversation with Zmicier Visniou who, among the icy wind, praises the grace of those very same high-rises; he speaks Belarusian, I speak Polish and Russian simultaneously, a rumbling. My relationship with Belarusian is a tram. My relationship with Belarusian snows. My relationship with Belarusian is an eddy that swirls into the gap between my neck and scarf, and melts.
        My relationship with Belarusian is a souvenir. My relationship with Belarusian is a walk with Volha Hapeeva, during which we speak German and English. My relationship with Belarusian is a praline shop on Francysca Skaryny Boulevard to which Volha Hapeeva takes me in wintry Minsk. My relationship with Belarusian is a parkour with lots of women who work in the praline shop and who all have their tasks to perform. In my relationship with Belarusian one woman takes the desired packet of pralines from the shelf, a second woman bags the packet, a third woman writes the bill, a fourth woman takes my money, a fifth woman hands me the bag, a sixth woman with brown-speckled fingers puts a sweet into my mouth. The last woman is invented. Although I know that this division of labour is an apparatus, a remnant of communist-bureaucratic times, I consider for a moment that my

relationship with Belarusian could be this praline shop. In that case the last, the invented, woman would be the poem that emerges when I and my relationship with Belarusian work on a translation together, which is a collaboration. My relationship with Belarusian recomposes the work of other women. And yet my relationship with Belarusian is neither necessarily feminine nor necessarily translation. My relationship with Belarusian knows many words which relate to "her" or "them." My relationship with Belarusian is always plural. My relationship with Belarusian is the opposite of an apparatus. My relationship with Belarusian fights bureaucracy. My relationship with Belarusian fights, with its border-crossing work, against a *generalissimo* who wants to dictate what the pralines ought to be called, in which language one ought to eat them, who can eat them, who must remain silent.

In the afternoon my relationship with Belarusian hums like a radiator. My relationship with Belarusian is warm. My relationship with Belarusian is a glove in a field in which animals live. My relationship with Belarusian is an interlinear translation with dashes and variants that reads like a hiking map, on it the field, the glove. All possibilities of expression are housed in it, disarrayed situations of saying, invisible layers under the fur. For that reason my relationship with Belarusian is multilingual. For that reason my relationship with Belarusian stutters: not because language is a peasant, as the *generalissimo* says, but because it's many pathways, channeling.

My relationship with Belarusian waves from the hotel window. My relationship with Belarusian waves its goodbye from the train window. My relationship with Belarusian changes trains. My relationship with Belarusian doesn't know a target language, only train stations in a transit room that grows through its translation-transfers. In America my relationship with Belarusian speaks English with Valzhyna Mort. It says: my relationship with Belarusian is a fuzzy beehive that buzzes elsewhere. I say: my relationship with Belarusian is not self-identical, not nationalist, it tastes sweet on the outside. My relationship with Belarusian is abuzz with second languages. My relationship with Belarusian is a flight of fancy. My relationship with

Belarusian translates Valzhyna Mort's poems, which are written in English. Valzhyna Mort's English poems are like an interlinear translation from Belarusian without an original. My relationship with Belarusian greets the absence of originals. My relationship with Belarusian is not at home. My relationship with Belarusian is double-tracked and never direct. When I translate Valzhyna Mort from English, then my relationship with Belarusian is interlaced and yet almost at home with itself. My relationship with Belarusian is an early train, a high-rise, a box of pralines. My relationship with Belarusian lies in the sleeping car facing backwards, drives across a bridge, is a bridge, hums.

Faux-Amis Footprints[1]

In German, if you lead someone down the garden path, you might tempt them to follow the wrong footprint: *auf eine falsche Fährte locken*. For me, translation becomes more and more such a footprint-following, in both senses of that phrase. On the one hand, it matters to me to walk alongside the original poem, i.e. to follow its running, striding, jumping more than its riddles, answers, and callings. I do not mean objectively countable metrical feet (although those too), but the rhythmic-kinaesthetic imprint which a line of verse leaves behind with its ups and downs, its cadences, in my body. Following the footprint of an English poem can mean, for example, not placing the verb at the end of a sentence (which is where all German verbs tend to go). It drives me crazy, as if Mark Twain himself sat on my neck: "German books are easy enough to read when you hold them before the looking-glass or stand on your head—so as to reverse the construction." That Mark Twain sits on my neck and doesn't breathe down it has something to do with the second aspect of the faux-footprint-following, namely, with mistakes, or with *im Nacken sitzen*, in other words, with the fact that something gets mixed up that translation normally neatly keeps apart. Secretly I dream of leaving behind the ideal of an orderly and clean translation and instead, at the point where nothing and anything goes, of playing with a certain messiness, which has long been wreaking havoc in my poems. A faux-amis translation. Which is *translantic*. A messiness that does not so much rely on inability (because you have to be able to make the better kinds of mistakes), but an inseparability. The pleasure of setting the foreign material to work poetically in the target language, like a shimmering lack/*Lack*. Maybe this messiness is just another word for what Édouard Glissant meant when he wrote: "To leave traces in language means to lay a trail into the unpredictable within the shared conditions of our lives." Unpredictable because following these forking paths of many footprints entails that sometimes you no longer know which side of the track you're on.

1

Translator's note: In the German text, Wolf's guiding conceit is to play with
the English idiom—"to lead someone down the garden path" as a false friend
of the German "in die Irre führen." In my English version, I have similarly
translated the German idiom "auf eine falsche Fährte locken" literally to match
Wolf's creative "translantic" process here.

Translating the Untraceable: On Ilse Aichinger[1]

There's going to be a departure, I'll be there, I won't miss
it, it won't be me, I'll be here, I'll say I'm far from here, it
won't be me …
Samuel Beckett, Texts for Nothing 3

In a 1982 interview, the Austrian writer and Holocaust survivor Ilse Aichinger was asked about the use of foreign words in her work. They're an opportunity, Aichinger replied, "to make language foreign to itself and to leave it alone in such a way that it must speak for itself again." Ten years earlier, Aichinger had published Schlechte Wörter (*Bad Words*), a small collection of prose pieces that are among the most experimental works of Austrian literature of the twentieth century. Rumor has it that it was because of this book that Aichinger was not awarded the Georg Büchner Preis, one of the most prestigious prizes for a German-language writer. In the title story, "Bad Words," the narrator announces her deep mistrust of supposedly "good" language: "I now no longer use the better words." Instead, she writes, "I'm beginning to have a weak spot for the second and third best," by which she means the overlooked words, language in the margins. The second part of the book consists of nine prose poems with short titles that seem to be in a language other than German, or rather, in a language that sounds foreign. One such title is "Galy Sad," of which at least one half is a familiar word, at least in English. But the title also seems to be a special kind of foreign phrase, because like "Hemlin" (another of Aichinger's titles) it works like a proper name. And names, as Yunte Huang suggests in an essay on "Chinese Whispers" and on the sound of foreignness in poetry, always remain concrete, distinct, and foreign; they are untranslatable into other languages.[2]

     In another prose poem with the title "Surrender," we read: "From now on I will rely on names only. On the names of hills, all types of names. I will try to act like someone who never arrives, someone untempted, someone untamed by any silhouette. Someone without trophies." The English title here is an actual English word. Or is it? Could it also be a name? If we squint a little and see words as things untamed by silhouettes, we might discover the German gerund of the verb "surren" (to whirr or to mutter) in that title. A gerund with the ending of a noun, of a person: "ein Surrender," someone who mutters or whirrs—an acoustic hallucination in the form of the proper name of someone who has not arrived in language, or who, just as you took note, already whirred away. What's more, the English verb "to whirr" can easily be misread as the German word "wirr," which means confused. "Ein Wirrender" would be someone who is lost, constantly in motion, and untraceable. Instead of finding the right word or the better word, the reader is left second-guessing, with a kind of double vision: surrendering to the word's fluidity. The foreignness of Aichinger's words, it appears, avouch a reality in these texts precisely through their otherness. They make language permeable but also ambiguous, which is maybe what the opening of the prose poem "Surrender" refers to: "I hear the work is done with tricks and traps, with membranes, permeable stuff—bright, hellish bright. But hell can be many things. It's hard to get through." Whoever wants to trace the outlines of Aichinger's bad words had better not come as a winner or a language dompteuse. These foreign words cannot be tamed when you meet them, and they cannot be colonized as a trophy.

The American poet Christian Hawkey and I have been working on a translation of <u>Bad Words</u> for over four years, navigating the tricks and traps of Aichinger's deliciously disorienting foreign language. When we gave the manuscript to poet and friend Pam Dick, she got back to us saying that the texts sounded like "the lovechild of Beckett and Robert Walser." Right on, we thought. And by the way, she asked, didn't we mean "Gaily Sad" in one of the titles? I shook my head and secretly wished it were so. Our friend remained skeptical and added that every English-language reader would consider "galy" a mistake, a typo. Oh, I thought, a mistake it certainly is. But more of a weaving mistake that foregrounds the structure of language and its permeability for other languages. A mistake which, in other words, makes writing possible in the first place. And more specifically, a writing that pays attention to loss, to silences, to the things that cannot ever be expressed with the "right" words, or coherent words. A writing of witness as "wirr-ness."

"Jenkins complained about the shortage of vowels. Every week they are misplaced," "Galy Sad" opens. Whoever thought for a moment that "Galy" was a typo for "Gaily," is now informed that the shortage of vowels is intrinsic to this writing. We don't know who Jenkins is, but he's out there, with us, a fellow soul in Aichinger's territory of defamiliarized language. For Aichinger, this process of defamiliarization, which "brings one's own words back to themselves," is the condition for any kind of writing that advances towards a reality and towards representing it critically.

But what does it mean for words to come round to themselves? Is it even true that language would then speak on its own? After all, such weaving mistakes are at bottom a (visual, tonal) stutter that remains unfinished, and when language stutters it always multiplies—in a state of possibility. This is why "galy," which in German sounds somewhat like "gallig," meaning acrid, will in English always—however subtly—contain its happy ghost "gaily," even though its "i" is forever misplaced. The word, one could say, is doubly foreign—not only because it has two ghost words in two different languages, but because it possibly even belongs to an unknown *and* to another language.

Aichinger has championed this dynamic and defamiliarized relationship with language in interviews and texts like "My language and I": "My language is one that tends towards foreign words. I choose them, I retrieve them from far away. But it is a small language. It doesn't reach far. All around, all around me, always all around and so forth." It reminds me of Jacques Derrida's *Monolingualism of the Other*, in which he writes about his complicated relationship with the French language as an Algerian Jew: "I have but one language—yet that language is not mine."

Derrida's famous statement reads like an intensified version of the slapstick picnic scene in Aichinger's "My language and I": "My language and I, we don't talk to each other, we have nothing to say to each other." While the claim to "have" a language always already represents a usurping, colonializing gesture for Derrida, the reality of a disowned language can only ever be represented "by playing with the non-identity with itself of all language" —by "playing and taking pleasure."3

For similar reasons, maybe Aichinger's <u>Bad Words</u> are written in a language that does not only tend towards foreign words but is characterized by being other-tongued per se. A language where words, by being left to "speak for themselves again," open up to the non-identity of all languages. And it is this opening that enables language to process and pay witness to the unsayable, and which transforms the bodily, linguistic, and existential experience of the extinction of European Jews during World War II into a constant poetic coming and going, disappearing and re-appearing of echoes, oscillating with the possibilities of the other language, which at heart consists of *several possible languages* that seem to build a web of tunnels under her work.

It's probably no accident that—in her own account—Aichinger read Beckett when she was writing these texts, as well as, interestingly, "notes on the idioms of English school children." The characteristic breathless-ness and centrifugal linguistic gestures of Aichinger's prose are also present in Beckett, especially in "Texts for Nothing," which Beckett translated from French into English himself. Even if those particular texts did not form part of Aichinger's reading, they seem to me—like the "i" in "galy"—to be tunnel-texts that are simultaneously pres-ent and absent underneath their original works.

Idioms, too, play a major role in <u>Bad Words</u>. In their informality and folksiness, idioms in any language are the epitome of being included, of belonging, of "having a say" in a matter, and because they require initiation and consensus, people want to be able to understand them. Aichinger withdraws from this totality of language by being other-tongued, in that she takes idioms at their word (like children might), or, to use a Benjaminian term, in that she de-forms (*ent-stellt*) them, i.e. through literal misunderstandings and defamiliarizations she makes new poetic routes available. In the prose poem "Consensus," well-known sayings or aphorisms, which in German are also called "winged words" (*geflügelte Worte*), are first taken at their word and then literally plucked apart: "The words of confluence, hey, words, poultry, separated before the time that has yet to be defined: when should your sweet eclipses have struck, when did they get into each other's hair?"

This bittersweet "separateness" in language, the double helix of gaily getting lost with ghost-words, gets to the heart of Aichinger's writing, i.e. the heart of a writing in the margins. It is also embodied in the eponymous heroine of "The Mouse"—a thoughtful observer who, in the end, sees her own disappearance as the strength of her existence: "Who knows, perhaps I rejoice because I am untraceable." To rejoice in reading Ilse Aichinger's other-tongued writing, in turn, means to translate into the present the untraceable in one's own language and in between languages, at every turning of the page. This process, rich in possibilities, brings reading closer to writing, almost as if one were to learn a new language that was not just different, but different for everyone. Why, for instance, didn't the misplaced "i" in "Galy Sad" disappear twice, I wonder? Then the "Gaily Said" of the unsaid would be the other-tongued trace of language in the place where it is not alone, but close to itself, gaily stuttering and untempted, the reclaimed trophy of bad words firmly in its hands.

NOTES

1

The quotations from Ilse Aichinger's work are taken from Bad Words, trans. by Uljana Wolf and Christian Hawkey (Seagull Books, 2018, forthcoming).

2

Yunte Huang, "Chinese Whispers," in The Sound of Poetry / The Poetry of Sound, ed. by Marjorie Perloff and Craig Dworkin (University of Chicago Press, 2009), pp. 53-59.

3

Jacques Derrida, Monolingualism of the Other or The Prosthesis of Origin. Translated by Patrick Mensah. Stanford University Press, 1998, p. 65.

Shakespeare 61

what is wakefulness in translation? spaces between words: not a blink, but clouds in the shape of sheep. count them. in German, tired eyelids are kept open with matches. a gap and they stick to it. with or without their red heads? certainly, a glow. a stick-up for sleep. and when, in this deep light, you rub against each word, tossing and turning, you will find another meaning shifting its shape every minute—*shadows like to thee, tenors* and *shames*. the tenor and shame of being haunted by another runs through this. but while shame is (not only when red) the gap between what's appropriate and desired, other and own, outside and in, a tenor can also be an exact copy or transcript. is wakefulness the attempt to create a copy of the other (the original) by constantly being alert, alive, by keeping one's eyes (words) open? or am i creating the other by refusing to take my eyes (words) off it? do you watch clouds change their shape, or do they watch you, shape you? translation is this lament: you are so far from me—transformed into a reversed lullaby. minutes grow into hours, hours into a wake. not over a dead body, but one that is so alive as to be constantly absent, slipping away, *far off, with others all too near*. being awake in translation means to trace this distance, but never close the gap (your eye, your mouth), to keep alive the far-off presence (lover, word). it's your language that haunts me and keeps me awake, and in turn my language watches yours, wanders always on your side (sight). in German, the words for wake and watch still show their common origin, share the same shape—*wach* and *Wache*—suggesting, perhaps, that being awake is a state that constantly needs to be guarded and reminded of its own alertness. gemeinsam, wachsam, or else, *idle hours*. what, then, is a watchman in translation? someone who lets the sheep slip past the matches. a shepherdess of *defeat* who intimately knows their desire to always be where *the others* are, closer to you. someone who knows that, if they ever arrived, language would finally go to sleep.

How to Subsister:
An Afterword

The poem may be said to reside in disrupted, dilated,
circulatory spaces, and it is the means by which one
translates and notates this provisional location that evokes,
prompts, and demonstrates agency—the ear by which
the measure by which the prosody by which to calibrate a
poetics that augments the liberatory potential of writing,
the storehouse of the human—
Myung Mi Kim 'Anacrusis', HOW2, I.2 (September, 1999), online.

Uljana Wolf's poetry cannot be seen outside her work as
a translator (of English and Polish poetry into German).
To translate, she writes, means to practice "transformations
and goodbyes." In its farewell to the original, translation,
or poetry that is informed by translation, also represents
a unique opportunity to question origins on more than
a textual level, and thus to partake in a political discourse.
Developing a poetry that engages with social issues,
Uljana's work demonstrates how contemporary hyphenated
identities can be expressed in poetry—by navigating the
silences in the maps of German–Polish history, as in her
first book *kochanie ich habe brot gekauft*, or so-called
grammatical and ideological "false friends" and immigrant
narratives in her second book *falsche freunde*, or ex-
ploring the multilingual subversions of historically patho-
logised "hysterical" women, of asylum seekers, and of
bi-lingual children in *meine schönste lengevitch*.
　　　Uljana and I both believe that translations of
poetry cannot attempt a pure or perfect congruence, but
must instead afford an investigation of the slippages,
moments of misunderstanding and ambiguity, from which
a new articulacy emerges. Uljana's work enacts the "pluri-
lingual poetics" that Caroline Bergvall detects in Rosmarie
Waldrop and Theresa Hak Kyung Cha, arguing that
"[d]isplacement is not here envisaged as exile but as the
very condition for a positive understanding of relocation

across and against the unifying, mythicized, and frequently exclusionary principles of national language and of mono-lingual culture."

Such a plurilingualism shows itself often by small modifications of a prefix, by swapping vowels, and by inserting unexpected consonants into words. Sometimes lines miss a full verb and have only the auxiliary, and since German grammar allows for the verb to appear at the end of a sentence, the syntactic guessing-game requires reading textual and contextual clues—always with a sense of dilation or semantic hovering. Since verb-placement at the end of a line is uncommon in English, I introduced other interruptions, absences, and disturbances of the otherwise often happily flowing and flip-flapping rhythm of Uljana's prosodic investigations.

Uljana's texts are often "written with" other texts; they appropriate and "transform" Sigmund Freud, Hélène Cixous, Gertrude Stein, Lewis Carroll, Susan Sontag, Stéphane Mallarmé, thus making the gesture of the connective 'with' in her collaborative-collagist practice emphatically clear. Texts are not isolated incidents; they can engender intertextual and real friendships—hospitable relations which she explores linguistically. It speaks for Uljana's generous poetics that she invites and acknow-ledges such continuities and dialogues—a conversation that translation, I hope, can further hospitably extend.

In translating Uljana's words I also extend our extra-textual friendship into text and vice versa. I am writing "with" her, in her words and in mine, and while I understand her (an adhesive for friendships), these trans-lations quite stickily and happily sound both like and unlike her. Translation becomes a work of transformed and transformative failure, a confrontation with impossibility, a giving up of mastery. These are familiar arguments from post-colonial critiques, and translingual translation itself becomes a driving agent in such a revision of mono-lingualism. Uljana's poems are rich in such a critique— are never just play despite or precisely because of their insistent interrogations of form and sound as side-kicks: they are equal partners in her translational poetics as politics. The poems resist the notion that one can ever be fully a "native speaker," fully own a language, be of it, within it, or on top of it. The "buzzing" train of my relationship with the German of Uljana Wolf is therefore, in her/my words, "double-tracked and never direct," it "lies in the sleeping car facing backwards, drives across a bridge, is a bridge, hums."

***

I'm grateful to Sophie for inviting my poems into this participatory, potential space called translation. Participatory because it is a multi-directional, open-ended process with the capacity to transform everyone and everything involved: poem, author, translator, reader. Yes, "a circulatory space:" On the page, a call and response, a choreography. Shared motions, notions: a ballroom. Me dancing with the translator, a twin of sorts, spinning self, but Sophie has her own moves, her own *mova**. How fun to be led and twirled and rewritten like that. And therefore, how utterly true to translate the title of the poem "doppelgeherrede" into "dancing double speech." The *walking* of the doppelganger finds itself transformed into something more fluid, *tanzen*, foregrounding an aspect already *present* in the poem, but opening it further, untying the bow, like a *Präsent*. And isn't that what it's all about.

     And so translation can make the work be seen— not as you would see it if you could read it with German in your head (if you'd been in that ballroom, *tingel tangel*, if you'd approached twin number one, playing the angles, talked to her, in Anglish, shared a cigarette, *oh wie net*)— but rather because that space never existed to begin with, in German, because she was always-already multiple, my language, was also twin number two, in that space, keeping up the pace, and twin number three and four, also on the floor—so that what you see in Sophie's translation is the work waltzing through that "interlace-space" between languages, charged by these movements even more so than when it was still German, which it never was.

*mova = language in Belarusian and Ukrainain

This participatory potential in translation surfaces perhaps most clearly in the series "subsisters," which gave our book its title. The whole series started out as what Sophie here calls an "investigation of slippages"—in translation, but also more generally in cultural transfers. It emerged from simple questions: What happens when you watch a movie in a foreign language with subtitles?[1] What marvelous and liberating incongruences might occur between what you hear and what you read—where what you see is never what you *get*? The series is comprised of seven sets of two prose poems. One prose poem is imagined as the "original version (*OV*)," mirrored on the facing page with an "original version with subtitle (*Original mit Untertitel, OmU*)." The second version picks up the language of the first poem, but slightly distorted, with words and images displaced, as if this were a movie seen through the eyes of a language learner, a foreigner, a squinter, or someone who got distracted reading the subtitles and therefore somehow misread the movie.

The imaginary "reader" of these movies, then, is the title's "subsister:" a clandestina who relates to the movies' actresses or heroines (all seven sets are based on American films of the 1940s and 1950s, some of them directed by Jewish-German refugees) as a sister, niece, or lover. Through her distorted reading, the heroines of the poems are transformed into strange sub-sets of themselves—less obedient, less coherent, with more messiness and desire.

Sophie decided to translate the squinting poetry of messy desire with a fantastic mixture of approximation and appropriation. She took the concept and "circumdanced" it, turning slippage into bilingual spillage. On the one hand, she translated the sets of poems more or less mirroring the distortions and word games between the German *OV* and *OmU*. On the other hand, she translated the concept, i.e. misreading and mistranslation as a poetic practice. She takes her own playfully faithful translation and uses it as a prompt for a third poem, adding her own "english version" to the mix. This third version is a poem is a poem in its own subsister-right, catapulting the original into its Benjaminian afterlife, or "ever re-renewed latest and most abundant flowering."

It feels important that Sophie and I are able to communicate as two speakers with the same mother tongue but traversed by different writing tongues; that Sophie's translation adds her English to the world from a position of subversion, of writing as nomad. Dancing with the translator, a twin squared. True to being left rewritten again and again, like that. And isn't it what that's all about.

NOTE

1

It might be helpful to highlight the different cultural practices regarding foreign-language films. While foreign-language films in the U.S. are subtitled, the majority of foreign films in Germany are dubbed by German voice actors. This practice developed after WWII and was encouraged by the American allies who believed the linguistic illusion created by dubbing would aid their program of denazification, essentially by promoting faster absorption of American cultural values. Some German cinemas show films in their original version either with German subtitles (abbreviated to OmU in cinema programs) or without subtitles (OV).

"**Annalogue on oranges**" and "**annalogue on flowers**" were written with: Gertrude Stein, Hélène Cixous, Lewis Carroll, John Huston, Susan Sontag, Stéphane Mallarmé, George du Maurier, and Bertha Pappenheim's own writings.

"**Subsisters**" was written with: Howard Hawks: The Big Sleep, Fritz Lang: Clash by Night, Douglas Sirk: All That Heaven Allows, Alfred Hitchcock: Lifeboat, Josef von Sternberg: Morocco, Douglas Sirk: Imitation of Life, Otto Preminger: Laura.

"**Böbrach**" is the name of a "home for asylum-seekers," located deep inside the Bavarian Forest. In 2011, it was criticized for its isolated location and its inhumane conditions.

"**Babeltrack**" was written with Roman Jakobson's "Child Language, Aphasia and Phonological Universals" on the island La Gomera.

ACKNOWLEDGMENTS

"from Babeltrack," published by Gulf Coast (Spring/Summer 2017).

"Dancing Double Speech," "speech, with a conjoined twin," and "second speech, with a conjoined twin" was published in STILL, 5 (2017)

"Stationary" and "Mittens" appeared in The White Review (2017).

"Can You Show Me on Se Mappe" and "Dust Bunnies vs Wool Mice" appeared in The Recluse (Summer 2016).

"On Classification in Language, a Feeble Reader I-III" appeared in New England Review (2016).

"Subsisters" appeared in Asymptote and won second prize in its Close Approximations Contest (April 2016).

"Subsisters: Lauren's Youngest Sister" was published by no man's land (November 2015) and New Books in German (Spring 2016). "Annalogue on Oranges" and "Böbrach" were published by PEN America (June 2014).

"Method Acting with Anna O.", "Böbrach," five poems from the "Babeltrack" sequence, and an earlier version of the "Translator's Afterword" were published in the chapbook i mean i dislike that fate that i was made to where (New York: Wonder, 2015).

"Shakespeare 61" was written in English for The Sonnets: Translating and Rewriting Shakespeare, ed. by Sharmila Cohen and Paul Legault (New York: Nightboat / Telephone Books, 2013).

Warm thanks to the magazines and editors who published this work.

***

The original German versions of the "Texts on Translation" were commissioned between 2010 and 2013, and appeared in the following publications:

"Faux-Amis Footprints" [Dirty Bird Translation] in: Newsletter of the Literary Translator's Union, VdÜ, Germany, 2010

"Messages from a Beehive" [Nachrichten aus einem Bienenstock] in: pARTisan, Minsk, Belarus 2012

"Translating the Untraceable" [Das Unauffindbare übersetzen] in: Ilse Aichinger: Behutsam kämpfen, ed. by Irene Fußl and Christa Gürtler (Würzburg: Königshausen & Neumann, 2013).

***

The translator wishes to thank PEN America for awarding her a PEN/Heim Translation Grant in 2015. She would also like to note that throughout the book her British spelling has been altered to American spelling.

Yoko Tawada's speech "On the Ellis Island of Language" was delivered on the occasion of Uljana Wolf being awarded the "Erlanger Prize for Poetry as Translation" in 2015. Many thanks to Yoko Tawada for the permission to translate and include the essay in an abridged version.

The German text of this edition is based on falsche freunde. Gedichte (Idstein/Berlin: kookbooks 2009) and meine schönste lengevitch: Gedichte (Idstein/Berlin: kookbooks, 2013). The publishers express their gratitude to kookbooks for permitting the republication of the original German poems.

INHALT

INHALT

Subsisters: Selected Poems
Uljana Wolf
Translated from the German by Sophie Seita

Copyright © 2017 Uljana Wolf and Sophie Seita
ISBN: 978-0-9885399-7-6
Designed by Jack Henrie Fisher

Belladonna* is a reading and publication series that
promotes the work of women writers who are adventurous,
experimental, politically involved, multiform, multicultural,
multi-gendered, impossible to define, delicious to talk
about, unpredictable, & dangerous with language.

Belladonna* is supported by funds granted by the Goethe
Institut, the National Endowment of the Arts, the New York
State Council on the Arts, the Leslie Scalapino — O Books
Fund, the Leaves of Grass Foundation, the Community
of Literary Magazines and Presses, and by generous
donations from individuals.

distributed by
Small Press Distribution
1341 Seventh Street
Berkeley, CA 94710
spdbooks.org

Belladonna*
925 Bergen Street, Suite 405
Brooklyn, NY 11238
belladonnaseries.org

Library of Congress Cataloging-in-Publication Data

Names: Wolf, Uljana, 1979- author. | Wolf, Uljana, 1979–
Falsche Freunde. English. | Wolf, Uljana, 1979– Meine
schèonste Lengevitch. English. Title: Subsisters : selected
poems / Uljana Wolf ; translated from the German by
Sophie Seita. Description: Brooklyn, New York : Belladonna
Collaborative, 2017. Identifiers: LCCN 2017014731 |
ISBN 9780988539976 (pbk. : alk. paper). Classification:
LCC PT2725.O433 A6 2017 | DDC 831/.92--dc23
LC record available at https://lccn.loc.gov/2017014731

* deadly nightshade, a cardiac and respiratory stimulant,
having purplish-red flowers and black berries.